P9-CNH-265

CAKE COUTURE

Modern Sugar-craft for the Stylish Baker

CAKE COUTURE

Modern Sugar-craft for the Stylish Baker

ANNIE DAM

FIREFLY BOOKS

A Firefly Book

Published by Firefly Books Ltd. 2011

Copyright Quintet Publishing © 2011

All rights reserved. No part of this publication may be reproduced, stored in a retrieval system, or transmitted in any form or by any means, electronic, mechanical, photocopying, recording or otherwise, without the prior written permission of the Publisher.

First printing

Publisher Cataloging-in-Publication Data (U.S.)
Dam, Annie.
      Cake couture : modern sugar-craft for the stylish baker / Annie Dam.
[144] p. : photos. ; cm.
Includes index.
Summary: Step-by-step guide with tips and tricks on designs for any occasion, including birthday and wedding cakes and cupcakes. Instructions and advice on ingredients, tools, baking, building, decorating, transporting, displaying and storing.
ISBN-13: 978-1-55407-949-0 (pbk.)
1. Cake decorating. 2. Icings, Cake. 3. Cake. I. Title.
641.8/653 dc22   TX771.2D36   2011

Library and Archives Canada Cataloguing in Publication
Dam, Annie
      Cake couture : modern sugar-craft for the stylish baker / Annie Dam.
Includes index.
ISBN 978-1-55407-949-0
1. Cake. 2. Cupcakes. 3. Cake decorating. 4. Cookbooks. I. Title.
TX771.D36 2011   641.8'653   C2011-904072-7

This book was conceived, designed and produced by Quintet Publishing Limited
The Old Brewery
6 Blundell Street
London N7 9BH, UK

Project Editor: Holly Willsher
Copyeditor: Cary Hull
Designers: The Urban Ant
Photographer: Maki Blazevski
Art Director: Michael Charles
Art Editor: Zoë White
Managing Editor: Donna Gregory
Publisher: Mark Searle

Published in the United States by
Firefly Books (U.S.) Inc.
P.O. Box 1338, Ellicott Station
Buffalo, New York 14205

Published in Canada by
Firefly Books Ltd.
66 Leek Crescent
Richmond Hill, Ontario L4B 1H1

Printed in China

CONTENTS

VIOLET SCROLLS
22

CUBE
26

JAPANESE-
INSPIRED TEA CAKE
30

BLACK & WHITE
RIBBONS
34

RIBBON ROSES
40

COSMOPOLITAN
44

GIFT BOX
48

RUFFLED BROOCH
56

POLKA DOTS
62

MARDI GRAS
68

MOSAIC
76

BAROQUE
80

BABY SHOWER
86

TOPSY-TURVY
94

FANCY CUSHION
100

ROSE BOUQUET
106

LUSTROUS PEACOCK
112

URBAN SAFARI
120

STREET SCENE
128

WEDDING GOWN
136

INTRODUCTION

I have always been fascinated by cake decorating and sugar-craft. It involves all forms of art, from sculpting to molding to painting. And not only is it pretty to look at, it is great to eat. Just remember that inspiration can come from all places.

Living with my parents as new immigrants in Canada, there were never any Western desserts in the house. I decided that I needed to take matters into my own hands and started to collect recipes for cakes, cookies, and ice cream. I remember trying to make chocolate mousse one day when my parents were out and having to hide whipped cream, eggs, and pans of melted chocolate when they came home unexpectedly. I didn't want them to discover my obsession with Western desserts.

During my years abroad in France and Spain, I had the opportunity to develop my real passion, combining art with my love for baking. As I perfected my style and learned new techniques, my cakes became more popular. I loved the feeling of everyone appreciating my art, and thus my career as a cake decorator was born.

The concept behind *Cake Couture* is to design beautiful edible art that makes everyone forget it is cake. The fact that our cakes become the center of attention at so many special and important events in people's lives pushes us to provide the most amazing creations.

In the following pages, I will guide you step by step, teaching you how to create beautiful cakes for your own special events. As you work through each project in this book, from the simple to the elaborate, you will begin to gain the skills and experience to design your own creations. The innovative designs and handy tips and tricks will transform the baking beginner into a confectionery expert.

It's very easy to adapt these designs to fit your special occasion. Each project can be personalized by adding your own touch of creativity. You can change the colors and experiment with the different decorating techniques featured throughout the book to achieve a more personal design. Use the original projects as a launching pad and make something really wonderful for your loved ones. Just allow your imagination to run wild and enjoy yourself. Your cake can become a real work of edible art.

Have fun looking through all the projects and get ready to be inspired!

CAKE DECORATING MATERIALS

> To decorate a cake, such as the ones in this book, you will need specific materials – beginning with the cake itself.

Cakes, Buttercream Frosting, & Royal Icing

You can make any flavor of cake you want for any of the designs in this book. Recipes for three cakes—vanilla sponge, chocolate sponge, and carrot—are on pages 12–13. Buttercream frosting is ideal for cake decorating and delicious to eat, and royal icing is used for attaching decorations to cakes. Recipes are on pages 14–15.

Fondant

Fondant comes ready to use and is sold in pails. Details on working with fondant are on page 18. Working with fondant requires cornstarch for rolling it out or for dusting your cutting tools. Occasionally you'll find that the fondant has become too dry, so you can knead a little shortening into it to soften it.

Food Colorings & Decorations

For coloring fondant, buttercream, and royal icing, I like to use gel food coloring because the colors are more concentrated and I can create any shade I want.

Sometimes I use a thin colored stain to obtain a more transparent color. For example, a brown stain gives the look of real wood, so I mix a little vodka with a food coloring to obtain the desired consistency. The alcohol evaporates quickly and will not dissolve the fondant.

There are many wonderful edible decorations on the market. I often use dragées, small beads of sugar that come in silver, gold, copper, or rainbow-colored; alternatively, if these are not available, you can make the beads from fondant, allow them to harden, and then cover with edible glitter, edible gold, or silver leaf. Luster dust is an edible dust that can be brushed on dry to add sparkle or mixed with vodka to give a more intense sheen. If luster dust is not available you can substitute edible glitter to achieve the same effect. Petal dust is a matte edible dust that can be brushed on dry to enhance the color of flowers or leaves or mixed with vodka to paint on details.

Other Supplies

You will occasionally need gum paste, for making flowers or any delicate decorations, such as feathers. When using gum paste, you'll need a bit of shortening because it can dry out quickly. Piping gel is used to adhere fondant to cake drums and as a glaze to add sheen.

CAKE DECORATING TOOLS

Once you begin to decorate cakes, you'll find you need specific tools to make the process easier. The most important and common tools are described below, but you will also find others mentioned in the design projects in this book.

Cake Pans, Boards, Drums, & Stands

Cake pans come in all shapes and sizes. I like to keep a wide range of metal pans on hand to have more to choose from. Cake boards are used under all cake layers. Cake drums are used to transport the cake. You will need them in several sizes and shapes. Finished cakes can be displayed on a decorated cake drum or a pretty cake stand.

Tools for Fondant

Large rolling pins are used to roll out large pieces of fondant to cover cakes. Small rolling pins are for smaller decoration pieces. Textured rolling pins have designs imprinted on them, which create fun designs. Fondant smoothers will help to ease out wrinkles and any air pockets. Sugar-craft guns also known as extruders create shaped pieces of fondant.

You can also find fondant tool sets that include veining tools for texturing, a ball tool for indenting, round sticks to thin out edges, a small palette knife for scoring, and a fondant ribbon cutter to cut strips of fondant to any width.

Knives

Knives are very useful in cake decorating. Large serrated knives are great for working on cakes—for leveling the tops, trimming the sides, and for slicing a layer in half horizontally. Pizza cutters are handy for trimming excess fondant from a cake. For more precise detailing, small sharp knives and utility knives are essential.

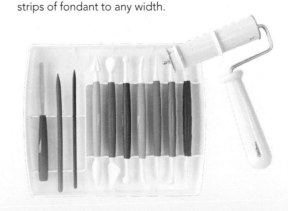

Design Tools and Cutters

Paintbrushes in several sizes are key tools for a variety of tasks; they'll help with the smallest details. A painter's palette is used for mixing colors. You can create amazing effects with an airbrush. It produces a very even coverage of color. You can add all sorts of textures with different tools, such as a quilting tool. Flower formers help you dry sugar flowers in a more natural shape.

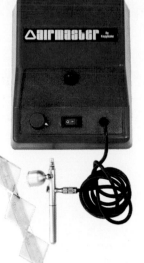

Cutters, mostly used for cutting fondant shapes for decorations, can be found in all shapes and sizes in cake decorating supply stores. Circles, squares, diamonds, stars, hearts, letters, leaves, flowers, and ovals abound. Having a large selection is useful as well as fun.

For stacking tiers, you'll need wooden dowels, which you'll cut with shears, and a pencil sharpener to sharpen one end of the dowel. Dowels are sold in ¼-inch (6 mm) diameter rods at cake decorating supply stores. The ones sold at hardware stores are not food-safe. Piping bags and assorted piping tips are used to add piped buttercream designs to your cake.

Other Useful Tools & Supplies

A turntable is helpful for holding the cake while you apply buttercream. Offset spatulas are wonderful for spreading buttercream frosting over a cake. Use dough scrapers to smooth the buttercream before laying on the fondant. Pastry brushes are used to apply piping gel to adhere fondant to a cake drum. Cookie sheets, covered with parchment paper, are useful to hold pieces of fondant as they dry. Toothpicks can help hold decorating pieces on the cake. Plastic wrap is essential for wrapping fondant when you're not using it. A thin piece of foam helps when you're working with some types of decorations.

BASIC RECIPES

Nothing is more disappointing than to cut into a beautiful cake and take your first bite only to find it dry and tasteless. I believe that a cake must taste as good as it looks. The following recipes have been perfected over the years, and their moistness and flavor are guaranteed to please.

BATTER AMOUNT TO FILL CAKE PAN

6-inch (15 cm) pan – 3 cups (750 ml)   10-inch (25 cm) pan – 8 cups (2 L)

8-inch (20 cm) pan – 5 cups (1.25 L)   12-inch (30 cm) pan – 11 cups (2.75 L)

VANILLA SPONGE
MAKES 6 CUPS (1.5 L)

This classic recipe yields a versatile cake that can be paired with any type of filling. The addition of beaten egg whites gives the cake a light, airy texture, hence the name "sponge" cake. To obtain this soft texture, avoid overmixing. Lightly folding in the egg whites will help to aerate the batter.

3½ cups (875 ml) cake flour
1½ tbsp. (22 ml) baking powder
1½ tsp. (7 ml) salt
1 cup (250 ml) whole milk
1 tsp. (5 ml) vanilla extract
1 cup (250 ml) unsalted butter
1½ cups (375 ml) superfine
 sugar
5 large egg whites

STEP 1
Preheat oven to 350°F (175°C). Generously grease two 8-inch (20 cm) cake pans. Set aside.

STEP 2
Whisk together the flour, baking powder, and salt in a mixing bowl. In a separate bowl, stir together the milk and vanilla.

STEP 3
In the large mixing bowl, cream the butter and sugar together with a handheld mixer until pale in color. Add the dry ingredients in three batches, alternating with the liquid ingredients. Begin and end with the dry ingredients. Mix until well combined.

STEP 4
Beat the egg whites to obtain stiff peaks. Gently fold into the batter. Do not overmix. Divide the batter between the prepared pans.

STEP 5
Bake for 45 minutes or until a wooden skewer inserted into the center comes out clean. Remove from the oven and let cool in the pans on a rack.

CHOCOLATE SPONGE
MAKES 6 CUPS (1.5 L)

The dark cocoa powder lends a good, rich flavor to this cake.

2½ cups (625 ml) cake flour
½ cup (125 ml) unsweetened cocoa powder
1½ tbsp. (22 ml) baking powder
1½ tsp. (7 ml) salt
1 cup (250 ml) whole milk
1 tsp. (5 ml) vanilla extract
1 cup (250 ml) unsalted butter
1½ cups (375 ml) superfine sugar
5 large egg whites

STEP 1
Preheat oven to 350°F (175°C). Generously grease two 8-inch (20 cm) cake pans. Set aside.

STEP 2
Whisk together the flour, cocoa, baking powder, and salt in a mixing bowl. In a separate bowl, stir together the milk and vanilla.

STEP 3
In a large mixing bowl, beat the butter and sugar together until pale in color. Add the dry ingredients in three batches, alternating with the liquid ingredients. Begin and end with the dry ingredients. Mix until combined.

STEP 4
Beat the egg whites until stiff peaks form. Gently fold into the batter. Do not overmix. Divide the batter between the prepared pans.

STEP 5
Bake for 45 minutes or until a wooden skewer inserted into the center comes out clean. Remove from the oven and let cool in the pans on a rack.

CARROT CAKE
MAKES 6 CUPS (1.5 L)

The tangy buttermilk in this recipe will make this the most moist carrot cake you have ever tasted. When I pair it with our creamy buttercream, our customers cannot get enough of this classic cake.

3 cups (750 ml) cake flour
2 tbsp. (30 ml) baking powder
½ tsp. (2 ml) salt
1 tsp. (5 ml) ground cinnamon
1 lb. (455 g) carrots, peeled and grated
3 large eggs
½ cup (125 ml) buttermilk
1½ cups (375 ml) superfine sugar
1 cup (250 ml) vegetable oil
1 tsp. (5 ml) vanilla extract

STEP 1
Preheat oven to 350°F (175°C). Generously grease two 8-inch (20 cm) pans. Set aside.

STEP 2
Sift the flour, baking powder, salt, and cinnamon together into a mixing bowl.

STEP 3
In a separate bowl, mix together the grated carrots, eggs, buttermilk, sugar, oil, and vanilla.

STEP 4
Gently fold the dry ingredients into the carrot mixture. Mix until combined. Divide the batter between the prepared pans.

STEP 5
Bake for 45 minutes or until a wooden skewer inserted into the center comes out clean. Remove from the oven and let cool in the pans on a rack.

BUTTERCREAM FROSTING
MAKES 12 CUPS (5 L)

Buttercream is a type of frosting that is used inside cakes as a filling, outside as a coating, and also for decorating. This recipe calls for butter to be added to whipped meringue, making a frosting that is as light as whipped cream. Buttercream can be tinted with gel food coloring; mix in a very little at a time until the desired shade is obtained.

2½ cups (625 ml) superfine sugar
12 large egg whites
5 cups (1.25 L, or 10 sticks) unsalted butter, cut into cubes
1 tsp. (5 ml) clear vanilla extract (available in cake decorating supply stores)

STEP 1
Mix together the sugar and egg whites in a heatproof bowl. Set over a pan of simmering water.

STEP 2
Beat with a hand-held mixer until the mixture reaches 140°F (60°C), and then immediately remove the bowl from the heat.

STEP 3
Continue beating with the mixer on high speed until the mixture forms stiff peaks.

STEP 4
Begin adding the butter, cube by cube. Beat until well combined, and then add the vanilla and mix well again.

STEP 5
If not using immediately, keep it well covered in the refrigerator. It can be stored for up to a week, but keep it away from strong odors as it may absorb the odor.

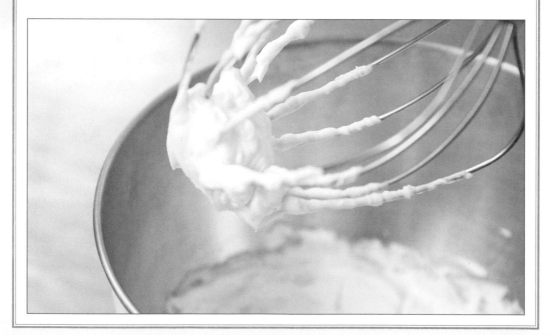

ROYAL ICING
MAKES 2 CUPS (500 ML)

Royal icing is a white icing that dries hard and is perfect for gluing decorations onto a cake. It crusts over quickly when left, so it needs to be wrapped tightly with plastic wrap until ready to use. If you want to color royal icing, use gel food coloring.

3 cups (750 ml) confectioners' sugar
2 large egg whites
1 tsp. (5 ml) freshly squeezed lemon juice

STEP 1
Sift the confectioners' sugar into a bowl.

STEP 2
Using a hand-held or stationary mixer, beat in the egg whites and lemon juice. Continue beating until the icing holds its shape when you run a knife through it.

STEP 3
Cover the bowl with plastic wrap to prevent the icing from drying out. Set aside until ready to use.

Royal icing can be used to embellish the cake as well as to attach fondant decorations.

ESSENTIAL DECORATING TECHNIQUES

LEVELING, SPLITTING, AND FILLING CAKE LAYERS

STEP 1

After you have made your cakes, allow them to cool completely overnight in their pans; the cake will be more firm, which will make the cakes easier to decorate.

STEP 2

Place a cake board of the same size and shape as the cake on top of a bigger cake drum. The drum should be at least 2 inches (5 cm) bigger than the cake for easy handling.

STEP 3

Place a dab of buttercream on the board to keep the cake from moving around. Remove one cake layer from its pan. Place it on the cake board, bottom-side down. Using a large serrated knife, level off the cake's rounded top. This will give the next tier a flat surface to sit on.

STEP 4

Now split the cake in half horizontally. Hold a large serrated knife against the side of the cake, and, applying gentle pressure, work the knife through the cake. Hold the knife steady so that the two halves are even. Lift off the top half and set it aside.

STEP 5

With an offset spatula, spread some buttercream over the bottom half. You want the buttercream filling to be about ⅓ inch (8 mm) thick and evenly spread right to the edge. Replace the top half. Place the cake on a turntable.

STEP 6

Apply a thin coat of buttercream to the top and the sides of the cake. Refrigerate until firm. This will seal in the crumbs and may take around 20 minutes.

STEP 7

Apply a second coat of buttercream to the top and sides of the cake. Holding a dough scraper flat against the side of the cake, turn the cake to remove the excess buttercream and smooth out the remaining buttercream. Refrigerate for 1 hour before decorating to allow the buttercream to firm up.

STEP 8

Repeat the process with each of the cake layers.

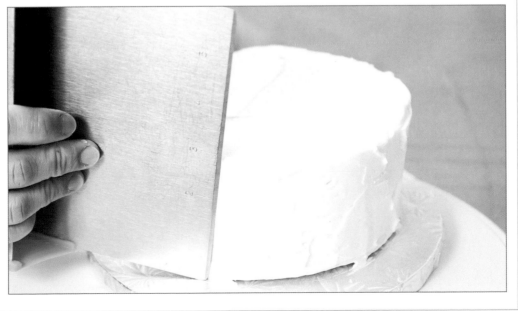

USING FONDANT

STEP 1

Fondant is applied after the buttercream is firm and acts as a great canvas for decorating a cake. It does not melt like buttercream, and it provides many more decorating possibilities. Fondant is also good for sealing in moisture, so it keeps the cake from drying out. The layer of buttercream underneath helps the fondant adhere to the cake.

STEP 2

Fondant must be soft and pliable and at room temperature so you can roll it out or color it. Knead it with your hands, to warm it up, until it is fully pliable.

STEP 3

If you're using the fondant in its basic color—white— you're now ready to roll it out. Skip to step 5.

STEP 4

If you're coloring the fondant, apply a little gel food coloring with a toothpick to the fondant right after you knead it. It is better to add a little coloring at a time so that you can control the shade of the color. Gel food colors are more concentrated and will not soften the fondant too much, as liquid colors do. If the fondant becomes sticky from the gel food coloring as you're kneading it in, dust your hands with cornstarch.

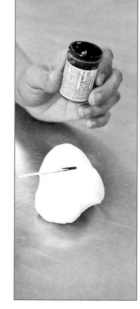

When the desired color is achieved, wrap the fondant tightly with plastic wrap and set aside until you are ready to use it. It is important to keep fondant tightly wrapped and at room temperature to keep it from drying and cracking. Repeat until you've colored all the fondant you'll be using.

STEP 5

To roll out fondant, take the amount of fondant you will need to cover the sides and top of a cake. Dust your work surface with cornstarch to keep the fondant from sticking. Using a large rolling pin, roll out the fondant to ¼ inch (6 mm) thick in the size you need. Remove air bubbles by pricking them with a straight pin to release the air. Make sure to continue dusting the work surface with cornstarch as you roll.

STEP 6

Gently lift the fondant by placing both hands underneath it, and place it over the prepared cake tier.

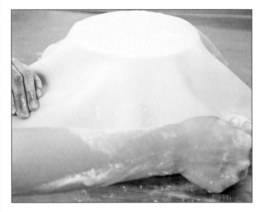

STEP 7

Ease out all wrinkles and air bubbles with your hands. Then use a fondant smoother to smooth the top and sides.

STEP 8

Cut off the excess with a pizza cutter. Save any excess fondant that has not touched the buttercream, wrap it tightly with plastic wrap, and set it aside for later use.

STEP 9

If you're using fondant for individual decorations, roll it to a ⅛-inch (3 mm) thickness. You can now cut it with shaped cutters or a fondant ribbon cutter, dusting the tools with cornstarch as necessary. Fondant decorations can be attached to a cake with a little water.

STEP 10

Sometimes fondant is used to decorate a cake drum, to match the cake. The process is essentially the same—you're using ¼-inch (6 mm) thick fondant. To trim off the excess, use a sharp knife.

STACKING CAKE TIERS

To make a tiered cake, you need to know how to stack and stabilize the tiers so they do not collapse under the weight of the tiers on top. You do this by inserting dowels into the lower tiers of a cake to bear the weight of the upper tiers. I like to use ¼-inch (6 mm) wide wooden dowels, which are sold in cake decorating supply stores (they're food-safe). You'll first need to cut them with shears or very strong scissors to the correct length.

The dowels need to be the exact same height as the cake tier they're going into, and you'll need enough of them to support the weight of the next tier. (Each project in this book specifies how many dowels and what length you'll need.)

STEP 1
Start with the bottom tier, which you've set on a cake drum. Cut the rods needed for that tier according to the instructions given in the project.

STEP 2
Center a cake board the same size as the tier above on the tier you wish to dowel. With a knife, lightly score the outline of the cake board. Remove the board. Working inside that outline, start inserting the dowels vertically into the cake, pushing them all the way down to the cake drum, and spacing them evenly within the imprinted outline.

STEP 3

Place the cake board back on the cake; line it up with the outline. Center the next tier, on its cake board, on the cake.

STEP 4

Repeat this process with every tier, except for the top tier.

STEP 5

The last step is to stabilize the tiers with an additional center dowel to keep them from shifting. Cut one long dowel to the length indicated in the project. With a pencil sharpener (that you have never used to sharpen a pencil), sharpen one end of the rod. Drive the rod, sharp end down, through the center of the cake all the way to the cake drum. To do this, you may need to hit it with a small hammer. Dab on some royal icing to hide the hole in the top of the cake.

A NOTE ON TERMINOLOGY

Cake decorating terminology can be confusing. As you begin to explore the world of fondant modeling, you will come to realize that many terms are used interchangeably—by beginners and experts alike. For clarity and consistency, we have used the following terminology in this book:

Fondant: the core ingredient in gum paste and flower paste; used as an umbrella term to describe gum paste, flower paste and rolled fondant.
Gum paste: malleable, nonsticky medium used to make basic sugar shapes and nearly all the sugar models in this book.

VIOLET SCROLLS

The simple, timeless scrollwork in this design makes it a classic. Keep it to one tier for a small gathering or repeat the steps on several tiers for a large affair.

TOOLS

- serrated knife
- offset spatula
- 8-inch (20 cm) round cake board
- dough scraper
- rolling pin
- fondant smoother
- pizza cutter
- 10-inch (25 cm) round cake drum
- textured rolling pin
- fondant ribbon cutter
- piping bag and coupler
- #3 piping tip
- stencil with scroll design

MATERIALS

- 2 (8-inch/20 cm) round carrot cakes (2 inches/ 5 cm high)
- 3½ cups (875 ml) buttercream
- 25 oz. (700 g) white fondant
- gel food coloring—violet
- cornstarch
- royal icing

OVERVIEW

All steps can be completed in one day.

- Make the two cakes and set aside to cool (approx. 1 hr.)
- Level, split, fill, and assemble the two cakes (½ hr.)
- Cover with buttercream (1½ hrs., including refrigeration)
- Cover cake with fondant (½ hr.)
- Attach the imprinted fondant (10 mins.)
- Pipe the deep violet royal icing along the imprinted lines (½ hr.)
- Stencil the top of the cake (½ hr.)

two 8-inch (20 cm) round carrot cakes (2 inches/5 cm high)

STEP 1

Level the tops of the cakes, split in half horizontally, and fill between the layers with buttercream. Place a tier on the cake board. Cover with a thin layer of buttercream. Refrigerate for 20 minutes. Cover the top and sides with a second, thicker coat of butttercream. Smooth with the dough scraper and refrigerate for 1 hour.

STEP 2

Reserve 1 ounce (28 g) white fondant. Dye the rest light violet. Roll out to ¼ inch (6 mm) thick on a cornstarch-covered surface and cover the cake. Smooth with the fondant smoother and trim the excess with the pizza cutter. Transfer the cake to the cake drum, adding a dab of royal icing to hold the cake in place.

STEP 3

Roll out the reserved fondant to ⅛ inch (3 mm) thick. Gently roll over the fondant with the textured rolling pin to give it a scroll design.

STEP 4

Using the fondant ribbon cutter, cut out a strip of fondant ½ inch (1 cm) wide and long enough to wrap around the sides of the cake.

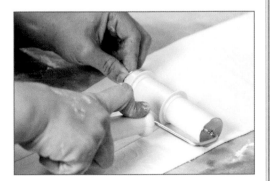

STEP 5

Attach the strip to the base of the cake with a little water.

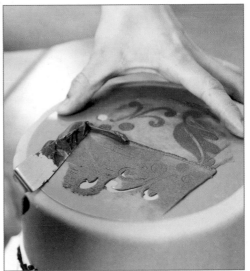

STEP 6

Dye ½ cup (125 ml) of royal icing deep violet. Fill the piping bag and attach the #3 piping tip. Pipe along the imprinted lines of the white fondant strip by holding the tip at a 45-degree angle to the cake and moving the tip downward as you apply pressure.

STEP 7

Place the stencil on top of the cake. Hold it still, and with a small offset spatula, spread a thin layer of deep violet royal icing over the stencil. Scrape off the excess. Gently lift off the stencil, without smudging the design.

CUBE

The versatility of this cake design makes it appropriate for people of all ages. Enjoy playing around with the colors and sizes of the dots.

TOOLS

- pastry brush
- rolling pin
- 10-inch (25 cm) square cake drum
- sharp knife
- plastic wrap
- serrated knife
- offset spatula
- 6-inch (15 cm) square cake board
- dough scraper
- fondant smoother
- pizza cutter
- 3 small round cutters in varying sizes
- ruler
- #12 piping tip
- black-and-gray striped ribbon
- glue stick

MATERIALS

- piping gel
- 30 oz. (850 g) white fondant
- gel food coloring – black
- 2 (6-inch/15 cm) square vanilla cakes (2 inches/ 5 cm high)
- 2 cups (500 ml) buttercream
- cornstarch
- royal icing

OVERVIEW

All steps can be completed in one day.

- Cover the cake drum with black fondant

- Make the two cakes and set aside to cool (approx. 1 hr.)

- Level, split, fill, and assemble the two cakes (½ hr.)

- Cover with buttercream (1½ hrs. including refrigeration)

- Cover cake with fondant (½ hr.)

- Cut out the dots and attach them to the cake (1 hr.)

two 6-inch (15 cm) square vanilla cakes (2 inches/ 5 cm high)

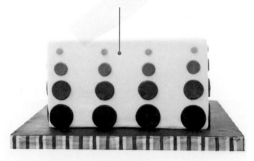

STEP 1

Spread piping gel evenly over the cake drum with the pastry brush. Dye 10 ounces (280 g) of the fondant black, roll it out to ¼ inch (6 mm) thick, and cover the cake drum. Trim the excess with the sharp knife. Set the trimmings aside and cover with plastic wrap.

STEP 2

Level the tops of each cake layer with the serrated knife, split them in half horizontally, and fill between each layer with buttercream. Stack the cakes on the 6-inch (15 cm) cake board. Spread with a thin coat of buttercream and refrigerate for 20 minutes. Cover with a second, thicker coat of buttercream, and smooth it with the dough scraper. Refrigerate for 1 hour.

STEP 3

Roll out the rest of the white fondant to ¼ inch (6 mm) thick and cover the cake. Smooth with the fondant smoother and trim off the excess with the pizza cutter. Transfer the covered cake to the prepared cake drum. Secure with a dab of royal icing.

STEP 4

Roll out the leftover black fondant you set aside to ⅛ inch (3 mm) thick, and cut out 16 dots with the biggest cutter.

STEP 5

Place the ruler against the base of the cake and mark at 1-inch (2.5 cm) intervals. Repeat on all sides. Attach the black dots using a little water within these 1-inch (2.5 cm) intervals.

STEP 6

Mix the scraps of black fondant with an equal part of white fondant to make a dark gray.

STEP 7

Roll out to ⅛ inch (3 mm) thick and cut 16 dots with the second-largest cutter.

STEP 8

Attach each dot directly above a black dot along the sides of the cake with a little water. You will now have two horizontal rows of dots.

STEP 9

Mix the remaining dark gray fondant with an equal part of white fondant to make a light gray color. Roll out to ⅛ inch (3 mm) thick and cut 16 dots with the smallest cutter. Attach these dots directly above the row of dark gray dots.

STEP 10

Finally, mix the remaining light gray fondant with an equal part of white fondant to make a lighter gray color. Roll out to ⅛ inch (3 mm) thick and cut 16 dots with the #12 piping tip. Attach these dots directly above the row of light gray dots.

STEP 11

Attach the ribbon to the cake drum with the glue stick.

JAPANESE-INSPIRED TEA CAKE

Inspiration for cake designs can come from all places. In this case, it comes in the form of a teapot. The delicate painted leaves and sugar bamboo against the fresh green makes this cake perfect for a spring celebration.

TOOLS

- 9-inch (23 cm) hexagon cake pan
- 10-inch (25 cm) round cake board
- scissors
- serrated knife
- offset spatula
- dough scraper
- rolling pin

- fondant smoother
- pizza cutter
- small palette knife
- painter's palette
- small paintbrushes and a big paintbrush
- small knife

MATERIALS

- 2 (9-inch/23 cm) hexagon carrot cakes (2 inches/ 5 cm high)
- 6 cups (1.5 L) buttercream
- 85 oz. (2.5 kg) white fondant
- food coloring—leaf green, chocolate brown, lemon yellow, and ivory
- royal icing
- brown petal dust
- vodka
- cornstarch
- small teapot to decorate top of cake

OVERVIEW

All steps can be completed in one day.

- Make the two cakes and set aside to cool (approx. 1 hr.)
- Level, split, fill, and assemble the two cakes (½ hr.)
- Cover with buttercream (1½ hrs., including refrigeration)
- Cover cake with fondant (½ hr.)

- Prepare, make, and attach the fondant "bamboo" pieces to the cake (1½ hrs.)
- Paint the sides of the cake (1 hr.)
- Final touches and additional decorations (1 hr.)

two 9-inch (23 cm) hexagon carrot cakes (2 inches/ 5 cm high)

STEP 1

Place the hexagon pan on top of the cake board and trace. Cut out the hexagon.

STEP 2

Level and split both hexagon cake layers and place on the hexagon cake board. Fill the layers with buttercream to get a 4-inch (10 cm) tall cake tower. Cover the top and sides with a thin layer of buttercream and refrigerate for 20 minutes. Spread a thicker layer of buttercream over the entire cake and smooth with the dough scraper. Chill for 1 hour.

STEP 3

Mix a small amount of the green, brown, and yellow food colorings into 36 ounces (1 kg) of the white fondant. Knead the fondant until you have a light pastel green color.

STEP 4

Roll out the light green fondant to ¼ inch (6 mm) thick and cover the hexagon-shaped cake. Smooth with the fondant smoother and trim the excess with the pizza cutter.

STEP 5

Using the small palette knife, gently score horizontal lines across the sides and top of the cake to give it a textured look.

STEP 6

Dye the remaining white fondant light brown. Measure out ½-teaspoon (2 ml) pieces of fondant. Using your fingers, roll each piece into 1½-inch (4 cm) long logs. Make sure you roll the center thinner than the ends. Holding each log on the vertical, lightly tap one end then the other against your work surface to flatten both ends.

STEP 7

Use a small paintbrush to dust brown petal dust over each end of the "bamboo" pieces. Attach the bamboo pieces to the edges of the cake with royal icing. Trim them if they are too long.

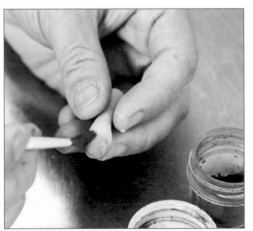

STEP 8

Mix the brown and green food colorings on the painter's palette and dilute with the vodka. With a fine-tipped brush, paint branches and leaves on the sides of the cake.

STEP 9

Dilute the color with some more vodka and lightly paint the edges of each side.

STEP 10

Make a diluted wash with the ivory food coloring and the vodka. Paint the top of the cake with a large brush. Decorate the teapot as desired and place it on the top of the cake when all the elements are dry.

BLACK & WHITE RIBBONS

Contemporary designs call for sharp contrast and clean lines.
The unique feature of this cake is the unusual heights of its tiers.

TOOLS

- 6-inch (15 cm) round cake board
- 2 (8-inch/20 cm) round cake boards
- serrated knife
- offset spatula
- plastic wrap
- dowels and shears
- 10-inch (25 cm) round cake board
- dough scraper
- rolling pin
- fondant smoother
- pizza cutter
- pencil sharpener
- 12-inch (30 cm) round cake drum
- clothing steamer
- big paintbrush

MATERIALS

- 2 (6-inch/15 cm) round vanilla cakes (2 inches/ 5 cm high)
- 1 (8-inch/20 cm) round vanilla cake (2 inches/ 5 cm high)
- 3 (10-inch/25 cm) round vanilla cakes (2 inches/ 5 cm high)
- 12 cups (3 L) buttercream
- 90 oz. (2.5 kg) white fondant
- gel food coloring – black
- cornstarch
- royal icing
- 3-inch (8 cm) wide black plastic ribbon

OVERVIEW

All steps can be completed in one day.

- Make the six cakes and set aside to cool (approx. 3 hrs.)
- Level, split, fill, and assemble each tier (1½ hrs.)
- Cover all tiers with buttercream (2 hrs., including refrigeration)
- Cover all tiers with fondant (1½ hrs.)
- Insert dowels and assemble the tiers (½ hr.)
- Attach ribbon to the bottom and top tiers (45 mins.)

two 6-inch (15 cm) round vanilla cakes (2 inches/5 cm high)

one 8-inch (20 cm) round vanilla cake (2 inches/5 cm high)

three 10-inch (25 cm) round vanilla cakes (2 inches/5 cm high)

STEP 1

Prepare the two top tiers (the 6 inch/15 cm and the 8 inch/20 cm), on its corresponding cake board by leveling the tops, splitting the layers in half horizontally, and filling between the layers with buttercream. Cover the bottom tier with a thin layer of buttercream. You will have one 4-inch (10 cm) high and 6-inch (15 cm) round tier and one 2-inch (5 cm) high and 8-inch (20 cm) round tier.

STEP 2

For the 10-inch (25 cm) tier, level the tops and split all three cake rounds in half horizontally. Fill between the layers with buttercream. Stack just two of the cake rounds (now on four layers of cake) on the 10-inch (25 cm) cake board.

STEP 3

Cut six 4-inch (10 cm) long dowels.

STEP 4

Insert the dowels vertically into the filled 10-inch (25 cm) cake. Spread a layer of buttercream over the top of the cake.

STEP 5

Place the remaining 8-inch (20 cm) round board in the center of the 10-inch (25 cm) tier. This will add support to the cake. Continue filling with buttercream and stacking the remaining 10-inch (25 cm) cake rounds. The result is a 10-inch (25 cm) tier measuring 6 inches (15 cm) in height. Spread a thin layer of buttercream over all three tiers. Refrigerate for 20 minutes. Cover the top and sides with a second coat of buttercream. Smooth with the dough scraper and refrigerate for 1 hour.

STEP 6

Dye 20 ounces (567 g) of the white fondant black. On a cornstarch-covered surface, roll the black fondant out to ¼ inch (6 mm) thick and cover the 8-inch (20 cm) round tier. Smooth with the fondant smoother and trim the excess with the pizza cutter. Cover the trimmings with plastic wrap and set aside.

STEP 7

Cut six 2-inch (5 cm) long dowels and eight 6-inch (15 cm) long dowels. Roll out the rest of the white fondant to ¼ inch (6 mm) thick and cover the 6-inch (15 cm) and 10-inch (25 cm) round tiers. Smooth with the fondant smoother and trim the excess with the pizza cutter. Insert the 2-inch (5 cm) long dowels vertically into the 8-inch (20 cm) tier. Leave a small space of 2 inches (5 cm) from the edge.

STEP 8

Insert eight 6-inch (15 cm) long dowels vertically into the 10-inch (25 cm) tier. Place the 10-inch (25 cm) tier on the cake drum, securing it with a dab of royal icing. Place a dab of royal icing on top of the dowels. Place the 8-inch (20 cm) tier on top of the 10-inch (25 cm) tier. Then place the 6-inch (15 cm) tier on top of the 8-inch (20 cm) tier. Sharpen one end of a 12-inch (30 cm) long dowel. Drive it vertically through the center of all three tiers. Cover the hole on top with royal icing.

STEP 9

With your fingers, shred the plastic ribbon. It will not shred evenly—there will be longer and shorter pieces, some thick and some thin. This will create a stunning effect.

STEP 10

Using a clothing steamer, steam all the tiers to produce a shiny finish.

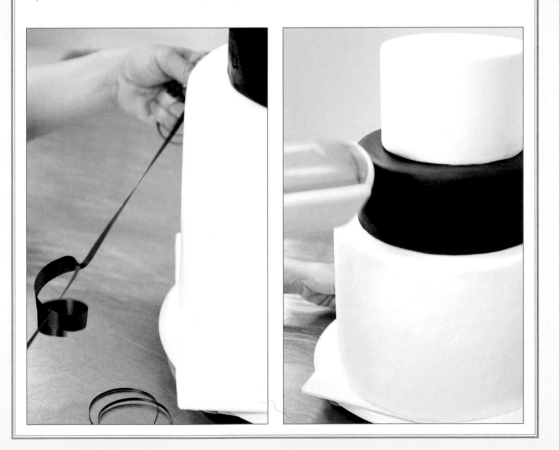

STEP 11

With a large paintbrush, wet the bottom half of the 6-inch (15 cm) tier and the bottom third of the 10-inch (25 cm) tier.

STEP 12

Encircle the wet sides of both tiers with the shredded ribbon, crisscrossing the ribbon. Steam again if desired.

RIBBON ROSES

This fresh and pretty three-tiered cake evokes the feeling of spring. You'll need to begin preparing the roses one day in advance to give them adequate drying time.

TOOLS

- parchment paper
- pencil and ruler
- scissors
- 3 piping bags and couplers
- 3 #102 piping tips
- #7 flower nail
- cookie sheets
- serrated knife
- 6-inch (15 cm) round cake board
- 8-inch (20 cm) round cake board
- 10-inch (25 cm) round cake board
- offset spatula
- dough scraper
- rolling pin
- fondant smoother
- pizza cutter
- dowels and shears
- cake stand
- pencil sharpener

MATERIALS

- 6 cups (1.5 L) royal icing
- gel food coloring—golden yellow, brown, ivory
- 2 (6-inch/15 cm) round vanilla cakes (2 inches/ 5 cm high)
- 2 (8-inch/20 cm) round vanilla cakes (2 inches/ 5 cm high)
- 2 (10-inch/25 cm) round vanilla cakes (2 inches/ 5 cm high)
- 11½ cups (2.875 L) buttercream
- 78 oz. (2.2 kg) white fondant
- cornstarch, for dusting

OVERVIEW

This cake will require two days to complete.

DAY ONE
- Prepare the royal icing roses in order to allow adequate drying time

DAT TWO
- Make the six cakes and set aside to cool (approx. 3 hrs.)

- Level, split, fill, and assemble each tier (1½ hrs.)

- Cover all tiers with buttercream (2 hrs., including refrigeration)

- Cover all tiers with fondant (1½ hrs.)

- Insert dowels and assemble the tiers (½ hr.)

- Attach the dried roses to the bottom and top tiers (45 mins.)

two 6-inch (15 cm) round vanilla cakes (2 inches/5 cm high)

two 8-inch (20 cm) round vanilla cakes (2 inches/5 cm high)

two 10-inch (25 cm) round vanilla cakes (2 inches/5 cm high)

STEP 1

Cut parchment paper into 2-inch (5 cm) squares. You'll be making several hundred roses, enough to cover the cake tiers, and each parchment square will hold a rose while it dries, so cut several hundred squares of parchment.

STEP 2

Fill one piping bag fitted with a #102 tip with 2 cups (500 ml) of white royal icing.

STEP 3

Dye 2½ cups (625 ml) of royal icing with yellow, brown, and ivory food colorings to create a muted golden-yellow color. Fill a second piping bag fitted with a #102 tip with 2 cups (500 ml) of that yellow icing.

STEP 4

Add the remaining white royal icing to the remaining ½ cup (125 ml) of the yellow icing to make a lighter shade of yellow. Fill the last piping bag.

STEP 5

Starting with the muted golden-yellow icing, glue a square of parchment to the flower nail with a dab of icing. Hold the bag at a 45-degree angle to the flower nail. As you squeeze out the icing, twirl the nail clockwise with your thumb and forefinger to form a rose. Stop twirling when the rose is the size you want.

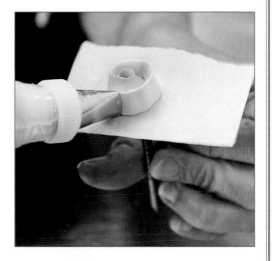

STEP 9

Dye the rest of the white fondant with the yellow, brown, and ivory food colorings to get a muted golden-yellow that matches the darker roses. Roll out to ¼ inch (6 mm) thick and cover the 6-inch (15 cm) tier. Smooth with the fondant smoother, and trim off the excess. Repeat with the 10-inch (25 cm) tier.

STEP 6

Gently lift off the parchment square and place it on the cookie sheet. Make roses of varying sizes until all the yellow icing is gone. Repeat with the lighter shade of yellow icing and the white icing. Let the roses dry overnight on the cookie sheets.

ASSEMBLING CAKE

STEP 7

Level the top of each 6-inch (15 cm) round, and then split them in half horizontally, creating a total of four layers. Fill between each layer with buttercream, and stack the four layers on the 6-inch (15 cm) cake board to create a 4-inch (10 cm) tall tower. Spread a thin coat of buttercream on the top and the sides. Refrigerate for 20 minutes, until it is firm. Spread a thicker coat of buttercream on the top and the sides. Smooth with the dough scraper. Refrigerate for 1 hour, until firm. Repeat these steps for the 8-inch (20 cm) and 10-inch (25 cm) rounds. Place each tier on its corresponding cake board.

STEP 8

Roll out 24 ounces (680 g) of white fondant to ¼ inch (6 mm) thick. Cover the 8-inch (20 cm) tier. Smooth with the fondant smoother, and trim off the excess with the pizza cutter.

STEP 10

Cut the dowels into fourteen 4-inch (10 cm) long pieces. Insert eight dowels vertically into the 10-inch (25 cm) tier and six dowels into the 8-inch (20 cm) tier. Space the dowels evenly. Place the 10-inch (25 cm) tier on the cake stand, and stack the 8-inch (20 cm) tier on top. Stack the 6-inch (15 cm) tier on top of the 8-inch (20 cm) tier. Sharpen one end of a 12-inch (30 cm) long dowel and drive it vertically through the center of all three tiers. Cover the hole on top with a dab of dark yellow royal icing.

STEP 11

Using small dabs of royal icing, attach the dried ribbon roses to the side of the 6-inch (15 cm) and 10-inch (25 cm) tiers. Alternate colors and sizes of roses.

COSMOPOLITAN

There is always an allure of excitement about New York City. This modern three-tiered cake pays tribute to the Big Apple and is perfect for a bridal shower.

TOOLS

- serrated knife
- 6-inch (15 cm) round cake board
- 7-inch (18 cm) round cake board
- 8-inch (20 cm) round cake board
- offset spatula
- dough scraper
- rolling pin
- fondant smoother
- pizza cutter
- plastic wrap
- dowels and shears
- pencil sharpener
- airbrush and compressor
- utility knife
- cookie sheet
- parchment paper
- paintbrushes
- piping bag and coupler
- #2 piping tip
- letter cutters ("I," "N," "Y")
- heart-shaped cutter

MATERIALS

- 2 (6-inch/15 cm) round vanilla cakes (2 inches/5 cm high)
- 2 (7-inch/18 cm) round vanilla cakes (2 inches/5 cm high)
- 2 (8-inch/20 cm) round vanilla cakes (2 inches/5 cm high)
- 7½ cups (1.875 L) buttercream
- 62 oz. (1.8 kg) white fondant
- cornstarch
- airbrush colors—pink, Hawaiian blue, black
- royal icing
- gel food coloring—black, red

OVERVIEW

All steps can be completed in one day.

- Make the six cakes and set aside to cool (approx. 3 hrs.)

- Level, split, fill, and assemble tiers (1½ hrs.)

- Cover all tiers with buttercream (1½ hrs., including refrigeration)

- Cover all tiers with fondant (1½ hrs.)

- Insert dowels and assemble the tiers (½ hr.)

- Spray the cake with pink, blue, and black airbrush colors (½ hr.)

- Prepare and make the fondant buildings and letters (approx. 2 hrs., including drying time)

- Attach fondant buildings and letters to the cake (½ hr.)

two 6-inch (15 cm) round vanilla cakes (2 inches/5 cm high)

two 7-inch (18 cm) round vanilla cakes (2 inches/5 cm high)

two 8-inch (20 cm) round vanilla cakes (2 inches/5 cm high)

STEP 1

Level the top of each 6-inch (15 cm) round, and then split them in half horizontally with the serrated knife, creating a total of four layers. Fill between each layer with buttercream, and stack the four layers on the 6-inch (15 cm) cake board to make a 4-inch (10 cm) tall tower. Spread a thin coat of buttercream on the top and the sides. Refrigerate for 20 minutes, until the buttercream is firm. Spread a thicker coat of buttercream on the top and the sides. Smooth with the dough scraper and refrigerate for 1 hour, until firm. Repeat these steps for the 7-inch (18 cm) and 8-inch (20 cm) rounds. Place each tier on its corresponding cake board.

STEP 2

Roll out the white fondant to ¼ inch (6 mm) thick. Cover the 6-inch (15 cm) tier. Smooth with the fondant smoother, and trim off the excess with the pizza cutter. Wrap the trimmings in plastic wrap and set aside. Repeat with the 7-inch (18 cm) and 8-inch (20 cm) tiers.

STEP 3

Cut the dowels into twelve 4-inch (10 cm) long pieces. Leave one dowel 12 inches (30 cm) long, and sharpen one end. Insert six dowels vertically into the 8-inch (20 cm) tier and six into the 7-inch (18 cm) tier. Space them evenly. Stack the 7-inch (18 cm) tier on top of the 8-inch (20 cm) tier and the 6-inch (15 cm) on top of the 7-inch (18 cm) tier. Drive the 12-inch (30 cm) dowel vertically through the center of all the tiers. Cover the hole on top with a dab of royal icing.

STEP 4

Fill the airbrush with the pink airbrush color. Spray pink onto the edges of the tiers, fading it out toward the middle of each tier. Lightly spray blue and black airbrush colors on top of the pink.

STEP 5

Roll out the remaining fondant to ¼ inch (6 mm) thick. With the utility knife, cut out building shapes, varying the sizes and heights of the buildings.

STEP 6

Place the shapes on a cookie sheet lined with parchment paper. Lightly airbrush with pink and blue colors. It looks best when the colors overlap slightly. Airbrush the edges with black. Allow to dry for 1 hour.

STEP 7

With a paintbrush, wet each "building" lightly with water on the unpainted side. Attach them to the top and bottom cake tiers. Overlap the buildings slightly and vary the heights of the buildings. With white royal icing in the piping bag and the #2 tip, pipe rows of dots to make windows.

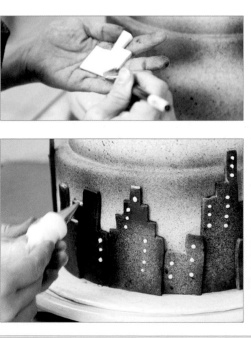

STEP 8

Dye 1 ounce (28 g) of fondant black and 1 ounce (28 g) of fondant red. Roll the black out to ⅛ inch (3 mm) thick. Cut out the letters "I" and "N" and "Y." Roll out the red fondant to ⅛ inch (3 mm) thick. Cut out a medium-sized heart. Attach the message "I ♥ NY" to the side of the middle tier with a little water.

GIFT BOX

The gift box is one of the most popular designs that we have seen over the years. You can change the colors, the polka dots to stripes, or the loopy bow to a traditional tied-up bow. Now you can have your gift and eat it too.

TOOLS

- pastry brush
- 8-inch (20 cm) square cake drum
- rolling pin
- sharp kitchen knife
- serrated knife
- cookie sheet
- parchment paper
- fondant ribbon cutter
- plastic wrap
- toothpicks
- small paintbrush
- 6-inch (15 cm) square cake board
- offset spatula
- dough scraper
- fondant smoother
- pizza cutter
- scissors
- small and medium circle cutters
- piping bag and coupler
- #16 piping tip

MATERIALS

- piping gel
- 72 oz. (2 kg) white fondant
- gel food coloring—leaf green, chocolate brown, lemon yellow
- shortening
- cornstarch
- 2 (6-inch/15 cm) square chocolate cakes (2 inches/ 5 cm high)
- 3 cups (750 ml) buttercream
- royal icing

OVERVIEW

This cake will require two days to complete.

DAY ONE
- Prepare and cover the cake drum (½ hr.)

- Prepare the fondant and make the loops (1 hr.)

DAY TWO
- Make the two cakes and set aside to cool (approx. 1 hr.)

- Level, split, fill, and assemble the cake (1 hr.)

- Cover the cake with buttercream (1½ hrs., including refrigeration)

- Cover with fondant (1 hr.)

- Prepare, make, and attach the fondant ribbons to the cake (½ hr.)

- Cut out and attach the circles and dots (45 mins.)

- Pipe royal icing along base of cake (10 mins.)

- Assemble the bow with the fondant loops and attach to the top of the cake (½ hr.)

two 6-inch (15 cm) square chocolate cakes (2 inches/5 cm high)

STEP 1

With the pastry brush, brush the cake drum with piping gel. Make sure to cover the surface completely so the fondant can adhere. With the rolling pin, roll out 18 ounces (510 g) of the white fondant to ¼ inch (6 mm) thick and cover the cake drum. Trim the sides with the kitchen knife and keep the trimmings with the rest of the white fondant. Set the cake drum aside to dry.

STEP 2

Cover the cookie sheet with parchment paper.

STEP 3

Mix the leaf-green, chocolate-brown, and lemon-yellow gel colors into 26 ounces (735 g) of the white fondant to achieve a sage-green color. Color 11 ounces (310 g) of the white fondant a deep chocolate brown. Leave the rest white. Set aside 24 ounces (680 g) of the sage green to cover the cake.

STEP 4

Grease a working surface with a little shortening. With the rolling pin, roll each of the green, brown, and white fondants into a ⅛-inch (3-mm) thick sheet. Using the fondant ribbon cutter, cut eight ¾-inch (2 cm) strips measuring 8 inches (20 cm) long from each sheet. Cover the remaining strips with plastic wrap and set aside.

STEP 5

Fold the fondant to form the loops. Break 12 toothpicks in half. With the paintbrush, wet the lower third of each fondant strip with a little water.

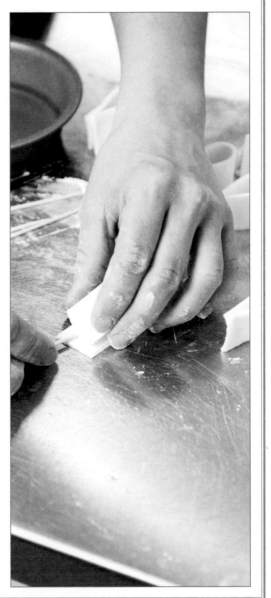

STEP 6

Lightly press one of the halved toothpicks into the wet part of a fondant strip, leaving half of the stick hanging off. Fold the strip over and pinch the two ends together so that the toothpick will not fall out. Set the loop on its side on the prepared cookie sheet. Use your fingers to shape it into a rounded loop.

STEP 7

Repeat with all the fondant strips. There will be extra loops in case of breakage. Set aside to dry on the cookie sheet overnight.

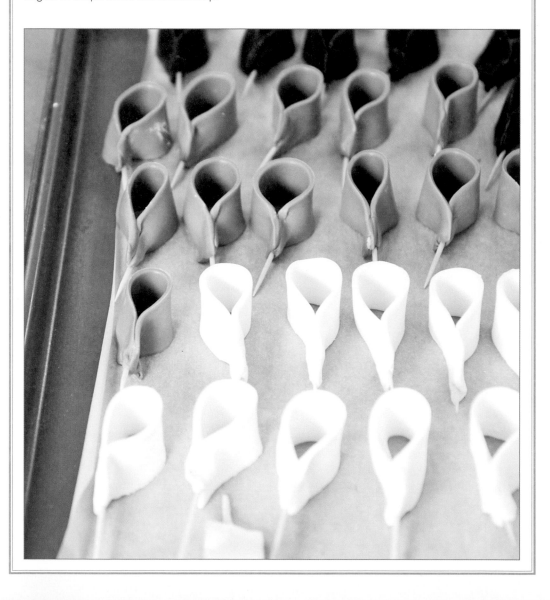

DECORATING THE GIFT BOX

STEP 8

Trim the tops of both cake layers with the serrated knife to achieve a level surface. Split each layer in half horizontally. Place both halves of one of the split layers on the cake board. Remove its top half. Using the offset spatula, spread ¼ cup (60 ml) of buttercream on the layer. Replace the top half of this layer. Spread the top with ¼ cup (60 ml) of buttercream. Repeat with the remaining cake layer and stack it, bottom-side up, on top of the other cake layer. Cover the top and sides of the cake tower with a thin coating of buttercream. Refrigerate until firm, and then apply a second coat of buttercream and smooth with a dough scraper. Refrigerate for 1 hour, until firm. Roll out the reserved 24-ounce (680 gram) piece of green fondant to ¼ inch (6 mm) thick.

STEP 9

Cover the prepared cake tower in the green fondant. Smooth all sides with the fondant smoother, and pinch the edges with your fingers to get nice, sharp corners.

STEP 10

Trim the excess with scissors and use a pizza cutter to trim around the cake. Transfer the covered cake onto the prepared cake drum, securing it with a dab of royal icing.

STEP 11

Roll out the remaining white fondant to ¼ inch (6 mm) thick. Cut out two strips, each 1½ inches (4 cm) wide and 16 inches (40 cm) long. Roll up each strip. This will make it easier to apply them to the cake.

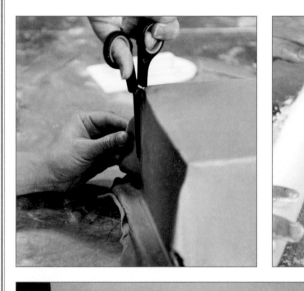

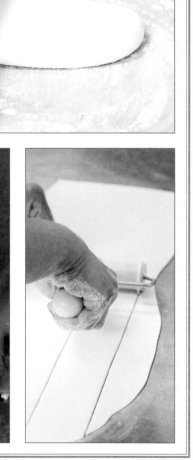

STEP 12

Using the paintbrush, wet the strips with a little water. Beginning on one side of the cake, apply the fondant strip to the center, rolling it up the side, across the top, and down the opposite side. Trim off the excess with the pizza cutter.

STEP 14

Roll out thinly any remaining white fondant, and then cut out circles with the medium circle cutter. With the small circle cutter, cut out the center of the medium circles.

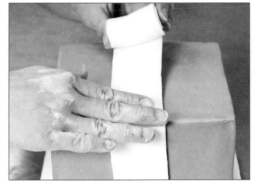

STEP 13

Repeat on the opposite side with the other strip. With your fingers, pinch the fondant together at the point where the two strips cross to simulate a real ribbon.

STEP 15

Moisten with the wet paintbrush and apply the medium circles randomly to the gift box. Repeat with the small white circles.

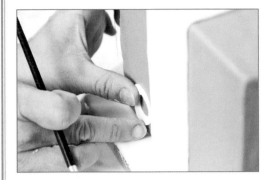

STEP 16

Thinly roll out the remaining brown fondant and cut out small round dots. Moisten the brown dots and apply to all the medium circles with the cut-out centers. Using the pastry bag and #16 pastry tip, pipe white royal icing all along the base of the gift box.

STEP 17

Roll a ½-inch (1 cm) ball of leftover green fondant. Insert the toothpick end of a dried fondant loop into the green ball of fondant. Working with one loop at a time and alternating the colors, cover the entire ball. The result will be a bow with white, brown, and green loops.

STEP 18

Gently lift the bow and secure it to the top of the gift box with some more royal icing.

RUFFLED BROOCH

This miniature cake proves that the old can be mixed with the new—with stunning results. Traditional ruffles and a cameo brooch are modernized by the graduated salmon tones.

TOOLS

- serrated knife
- offset spatula
- 5-inch (13 cm) round cake board
- 6-inch (15 cm) round cake board
- dough scraper
- small and large rolling pins
- fondant smoother
- pizza cutter
- plastic wrap
- medium oval cutter
- paintbrush
- 8-inch (20 cm) round cake drum
- dowels and shears
- cameo mold
- piece of thin foam
- rounded stick

MATERIALS

- 2 (5-inch/13 cm) round vanilla cakes (2 inches/ 5 cm high)
- 2 (6-inch/15 cm) round vanilla cakes (2 inches/ 5 cm high)
- 4 cups (1 L) buttercream
- 70 oz. (2 kg) ivory fondant
- gel food coloring—red, orange, brown
- cornstarch
- royal icing

OVERVIEW

This cake can be completed in one day due to its small size. For a larger version, allot yourself at least two days to cover completely with ruffles.

- Make the four cakes and set aside to cool (approx. 2 hrs.)
- Level, split, fill, and assemble the tiers (1 hr.)
- Cover each tier with buttercream (1½ hrs., including refrigeration)
- Cover the tiers with fondant and assemble (1 hr.)

- Prepare the fondant and make and attach the fondant ruffles to the bottom tier and to the top of the cake (approx. 2½ hrs.)
- Make and attach the brooch (15 mins.)

two 5-inch (13 cm) round vanilla cakes (2 inches/5 cm high)

two 6-inch (15 cm) round vanilla cakes (2 inches/5 cm high)

STEP 1

Prepare the tiers—each on its corresponding cake board—by leveling the tops of each cake round, splitting them horizontally, and filling between each layer with buttercream. Cover each tier with a thin layer of buttercream and refrigerate for 20 minutes. Cover with a second, thicker coat of buttercream and smooth with the dough scraper. Chill for 1 hour.

STEP 2

Roll out 40 ounces (1 kg) of the ivory fondant to ¼ inch (6 mm) thick and cover the tiers. Smooth with the fondant smoother and trim the excess with the pizza cutter.

STEP 3

Measure out 5 ounces (142 g) of the ivory fondant. Mix in red, orange, and brown food coloring to dye it a dark salmon color. Roll out to ⅛ inch (3 mm) thick. Using the medium oval cutter, cut out oval pieces.

STEP 4

Hold one oval piece in your hand and use your fingers to pinch the top half of the oval together to make a ruffled piece.

STEP 5

With a wet paintbrush, wet the ruffle piece and apply it to the base of the 6-inch (15 cm) tier. Repeat, attaching the ruffle pieces closely side by side, until the entire base is covered. Set the 6-inch (15 cm) tier aside and begin to cover the outside edge of the top of the 5-inch (13 cm) tier with more ruffles. The result will be a ring of dark salmon-colored ruffles, with the ruffles all facing out.

STEP 6

Mix an equal amount of ivory fondant with the remaining dark salmon fondant to lighten the color. Roll out to ⅛ inch (3 mm) thick and cut out ovals. Pinch the top half of the oval to make a ruffle. Continue mixing the fondant, creating lighter colored fondants each time by mixing equal parts ivory fondant with the colored fondants, cutting out ovals, and creating ruffles.

STEP 7

Attach each new color of ruffles to the tiers, working from bottom to top on the 6-inch (15 cm) tier and outside to inside on the top of the 5-inch (13 cm) tier. Leave a 5-inch (13 cm) diameter space on the top of the 6-inch (15 cm) tier. This is where the 5-inch (13 cm) tier will sit.

STEP 8

Place the 6-inch (15 cm) tier on top of the 8-inch (20 cm) cake drum, securing it in place with a dab of royal icing. Cut four pieces of dowel to 4 inches (10 cm) in length. Insert the dowels vertically into the center of the 6-inch (15 cm) tier, keeping them evenly spaced. Place a dab of royal icing on top of each dowel. Place the 5-inch (13 cm) tier on top of the dowels.

STEP 9

Roll out the remaining ivory fondant to ⅛ inch (3 mm) thick. Cut out one oval. Roll up the oval lengthwise to produce a small rosette. Place the rosette in the center of the 5-inch (13 cm) tier.

STEP 10

Press the remaining ivory fondant into the cameo mold.

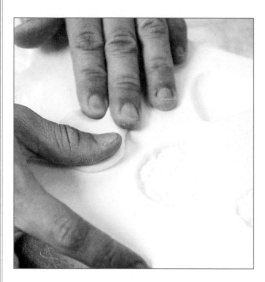

STEP 11

Roll out the leftover lightest salmon-colored fondant to ⅛ inch (3 mm) thick. Place it on the thin piece of foam and thin the edges with the rounded stick.

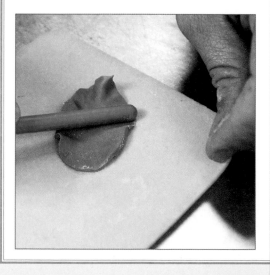

STEP 12

Unmold the cameo brooch. Attach it with a little water to the thinned-out oval. Attach the brooch and thinned-out oval to the side of the 5-inch (13 cm) tier.

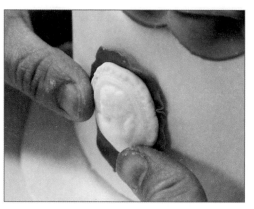

POLKA DOTS

The height of this sweet and simple cake makes it an eye-catching piece for a wedding. The ivory dots against the chocolate-brown background add a playful touch for the modern bride.

TOOLS

- serrated knife
- offset spatula
- 6-inch (15 cm) round cake board
- dough scraper
- 8-inch (20 cm) round cake board
- 10-inch (25 cm) round cake board
- 12-inch (30 cm) round cake board
- rolling pin
- fondant smoother
- pizza cutter
- dowels and shears
- 16-inch (40 cm) round cake drum
- pencil sharpener
- parchment paper
- scissors
- small knife
- small round cookie cutter
- small paintbrush

MATERIALS

- 2 (6-inch/15 cm) round chocolate cakes (2 inches/ 5 cm high)
- 2 (8-inch/20 cm) round chocolate cakes (2 inches/ 5 cm high)
- 2 (10-inch/25 cm) round chocolate cakes (2 inches/ 5 cm high)
- 2 (12-inch/30 cm) round chocolate cakes (2 inches/ 5 cm high)
- 20 cups (5 L) buttercream
- 126 oz. (3.5 kg) chocolate fondant
- 50 oz. (1.4 kg) white fondant
- gel food coloring – ivory
- cornstarch
- royal icing

OVERVIEW

This cake can be completed in one day.

- Make the eight cakes and set aside to cool (approx. 4 hrs.)

- Level, split, fill, and assemble the tiers (1½ hrs.)

- Cover each tier with buttercream (2 hrs., including refrigeration)

- Cover the tiers with fondant and assemble (2 hrs.)

- Prepare, make, and attach the fondant dots to all the tiers of the cake (approx. 1½ hrs.)

two 6-inch (15 cm) round chocolate cakes (2 inches/5 cm high)

two 10-inch (25 cm) round chocolate cakes (2 inches/5 cm high)

two 8-inch (20 cm) round chocolate cakes (2 inches/5 cm high)

two 12-inch (30 cm) round chocolate cakes (2 inches/5 cm high)

STEP 1

Level the top of each 6-inch (15 cm) round, and then split them in half horizontally, creating a total of four layers. Fill between each layer with buttercream and stack the four layers on the 6-inch (15 cm) round cake board to create a 4-inch (10 cm) tall tower. Spread a thin coat of buttercream on the top and the sides. Refrigerate for 20 minutes, until the buttercream is firm. Spread a thicker coat of buttercream on the top and the sides. Smooth with the dough scraper. Refrigerate for 1 hour, until firm. Repeat these steps for the 8-inch (20 cm), 10-inch (25 cm), and 12-inch (30 cm) rounds. Place each tier on its corresponding cake board.

STEP 2

On a cornstarch-covered surface, roll out the chocolate fondant to ⅛ inch (3 mm) thick. Cover each tier and smooth with the fondant smoother. Cut away the excess fondant with the pizza cutter.

STEP 3

Cut dowels into 4-inch (10 cm) long pieces. Set aside one 12-inch (30 cm) long dowel. Insert four short dowels vertically into the 8-inch (20 cm) tier, six in the 10-inch (25 cm) tier, and eight in the 12-inch (30 cm) tier. Make sure the dowels are evenly spaced and no less than 2 inches (5 cm) from the edge.

STEP 4

Place the 12-inch (30 cm) tier on the cake drum, along with a dab of royal icing to hold it in place. Place a dab of royal icing on top of each dowel. Stack the 10-inch (25 cm) tier on top of the 12-inch (30 cm) tier. Then stack the 8-inch (20 cm) tier on top of the 10-inch (25 cm) tier, and end by stacking the 6-inch (15 cm) tier on top of the 8-inch (20 cm) tier. Sharpen the 12-inch (30 cm) long dowel. Drive it vertically through the center of all four tiers to secure the cake together.

STEP 5

Cut a strip of parchment 3 inches (8 cm) wide and long enough to just go around the circumference of the 12-inch (30 cm) tier. Fold the strip in half.

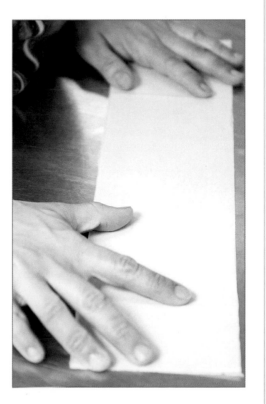

STEP 6

Continue folding the strip in half until it is about 2 inches (5 cm) long. Unfold.

STEP 7

Wrap the strip of parchment around the base of the 12-inch (30 cm) tier. The folded creases in the strip will be the guide to where the ivory dots will be placed. Mark these places with a knife along the base of the tier.

STEP 8

Mix the white fondant with the ivory food coloring. Knead it until the color is uniform. Roll out to ⅛ inch (3 mm) thick. Cut out dots with the small round cutter.

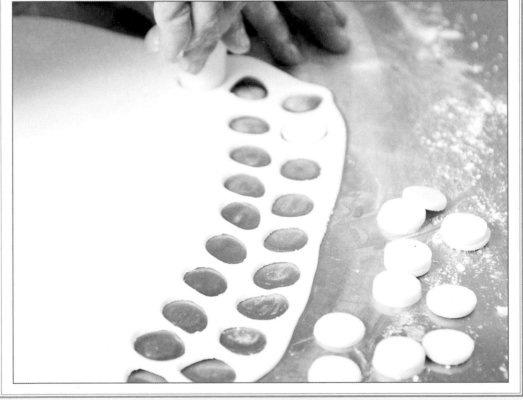

STEP 9

Lightly wet each dot with the paintbrush and attach it to the marked spots on the tier. Continue until you have a row of ivory dots along the bottom of the cake. Roll out the fondant remnants and cut out more dots. Add a second row of dots above the first row. Stagger the second row so the dots are not directly on top of each other. Make sure that the dots are evenly spaced. Continue these steps for a third row of dots. Repeat steps 5 onward for the remaining tiers.

MARDI GRAS

Capture the mystery and flair of Mardi Gras with this two-tiered cake.
The colors can be adjusted for a bolder or more subtle effect.
Your guests will be amazed that even the mask is edible. You will need to
start this cake three days in advance so the mask has enough time to dry.

TOOLS

- plastic wrap
- plastic craft mask
- rolling pin
- utility knife
- large and medium petal cutters
- medium circle cutter
- sugar-craft gun with medium circle attachment
- paintbrush
- 8-inch (20 cm) square cake board
- 12-inch (30 cm) square cake board
- serrated knife
- offset spatula
- dough scraper
- fondant smoother
- pizza cutter
- airbrush and compressor
- 16-inch (40 cm) cake drum
- dowels and shears
- piping bag and coupler
- #3, #18, and #101 piping tips

MATERIALS

- 160 oz. (4.5 kg) white fondant
- ½ tsp. (2 ml) gum tragacanth
- cornstarch
- gel food coloring—pink, purple, black
- silver luster dust or edible glitter
- vodka
- silver dragées or fondant balls
- 2 (8-inch/20 cm) square vanilla cakes (2 inches/ 5 cm high)
- 2 (12-inch/30 cm) square vanilla cakes (2 inches/ 5 cm high)
- 10 cups (2.5 L) buttercream
- airbrush color—violet
- royal icing
- black petal dust
- white Candy Melts
- feathers

OVERVIEW

This cake will require three days to complete.

DAY ONE
- Prepare the white fondant mask (1 hr.)

DAY THREE
- Make the four cakes and set aside to cool (approx. 2 hrs.)

- Level, split, fill, and assemble the tiers (½ hr.)

- Cover each tier with buttercream (1½ hrs., including refrigeration)

- Cover the tiers with fondant and assemble (1 hr.)

- Pipe the decorations onto the bottom and sides of each tier. Let dry then paint silver (approx. 2 hrs., including drying time)

- Decorate and attach the fondant mask (approx. 2 hrs.)

- Final touches (15 mins.)

two 8-inch (20 cm) square vanilla cakes (2 inches/5 cm high)

two 12-inch (30 cm) square vanilla cakes (2 inches/5 cm high)

THREE DAYS IN ADVANCE

STEP 1

The mask must be prepared three days in advance to have enough time to dry. Knead 20 ounces (567 g) of white fondant with the gum tragacanth. Mix well and wrap in plastic wrap. Set aside to rest for 15 minutes.

STEP 2

Cover the plastic craft mask with plastic wrap. On a surface dusted with cornstarch, roll out the prepared white fondant to ⅛ inch (3 mm) thick. Lay it over the mask and gently press with your fingers while following the contours.

STEP 3

With a utility knife, cut out the eyes and the edges by following the lines of the plastic mask. Allow this to dry for three days.

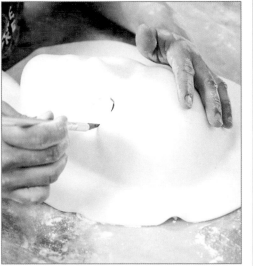

ASSEMBLING THE CAKE

STEP 4

Dye 30 ounces (850 g) of the white fondant a deep purple. Roll it out to ⅛ inch (3 mm) thick. With the large petal cutter, cut out a large petal. Attach it to the center of the forehead of the fondant mask with a little water.

STEP 5

Cut out a medium circle with the circle cutter. Measure it against the left eye of the mask and trim off a corner of the circle to form a crescent shape. Attach it to the left eye of the fondant mask with a little water.

STEP 6

Using the medium petal cutter as a guide, cut out the center of the purple petal that is attached to the fondant mask with the utility knife.

STEP 7

Dye 10 ounces (283 g) of the white fondant black. Fill a sugar-craft gun fitted with the medium circle attachment. Squeeze out a long string and attach it with a little water to the fondant mask, following the outlines of the purple fondant pieces. Attach two longer black strings to both sides of the fondant mask.

STEP 8

Using smaller pieces of the black string, create a pattern on the right cheek of the fondant mask and make a black eyebrow for the right eye.

STEP 9

Mix some silver luster dust or edible glitter with vodka. Paint the cut-out petal shape on the forehead of the fondant mask silver. Paint all the other black parts, except for the black eyebrow, silver. Apply silver dragées or fondant silver balls to the cheek design and purple pieces while the silver paint is still wet. Set aside to dry while you prepare the cake tiers.

STEP 10

Level the tops of the cakes, split each in half horizontally, fill each 8-inch (20 cm) and 12-inch (30 cm) tier, with each on its corresponding cake board. Cover each with a thin layer of buttercream. Chill for 20 minutes each then frost the cakes with a thicker coat of buttercream. Smooth with the dough scraper and refrigerate for 1 hour.

STEP 11

Dye 100 ounces (2.8 kg) of the white fondant a medium pink. Roll out to ¼ inch (6 mm) thick and cover the 12-inch (30 cm) square tier. Smooth with the fondant smoother and trim the excess with the pizza cutter. Repeat with the 8-inch (20 cm) square tier.

STEP 12

Fill the airbrush with the violet airbrush color. Starting with the 12-inch (30 cm) tier, lightly spray the edges of the entire cake to create depth. Repeat with the 8-inch (20 cm) square tier.

STEP 13

Transfer the 12-inch (30 cm) tier to the cake drum, staggering it on the drum so that the corners of the tier are situated at the center point of each side of the cake drum. Cut eight 4-inch (10 cm) long dowels. Insert the dowels vertically into the center of the 12-inch (30 cm) tier, keeping them evenly spaced. Place a dab of royal icing on top of each dowel. Place the 8-inch (20 cm) square tier on top of the 12-inch (30 cm) tier. Stagger it so that the corners of the 8-inch (20 cm) tier are situated at the midpoint of each side of the 12-inch (30 cm) tier.

STEP 14

Mix ½ cup (125 ml) of royal icing with the black petal dust to make it light gray. Fit the piping bag with the #3 piping tip and fill the bag with royal icing. Pipe branches onto all eight corners of the two-tiered cake. Change the tip to #101 and pipe leaves on the piped branches. Change the tip to #18 and pipe a border along the base of both tiers. Allow to dry for 1 hour.

STEP 15

Mix some silver luster dust or edible glitter with vodka. With a small paintbrush, carefully paint in all the branches, leaves, and piped border. Gently lift the fondant mask from the plastic mask underneath. Place the fondant mask on the cake, with the base of the mask resting on the 12-inch (30 cm) tier and the top resting against one flat side of the 8-inch (20 cm) tier. Secure with some melted white Candy Melts.

STEP 17

Dye ¼ cup (60 ml) of royal icing deep purple. Fill a piping bag fitted with the #3 tip and pipe a border around the edges of the fondant mask.

STEP 16

Attach five feathers to the top of the fondant mask, on the reverse side. Wrap the ends of the remaining feathers in plastic wrap. Insert half of the feathers into the top of the 12-inch (30 cm) tier, to the right of the fondant mask. Insert the remaining feathers into the left side of the 12-inch (30 cm) tier.

MOSAIC

The art of creating beautiful designs by assembling small pieces of colored tiles can be recreated in cake form. The different tones of blue against the stark white cake create a stunning effect.

TOOLS

- 6-inch (15 cm) round cake board
- 10-inch (25 cm) round cake board
- 12-inch (30 cm) round cake board
- serrated knife
- offset spatula
- dough scraper
- plastic wrap
- rolling pin
- fondant smoother
- pizza cutter
- dowels and shears
- pencil sharpener
- blue edible ink pen
- small square cutter
- utility knife
- small paintbrush
- cake stand

MATERIALS

- 2 (6-inch/15 cm) round vanilla cakes (2 inches/ 5 cm high)
- 2 (10-inch/25 cm) round vanilla cakes (2 inches/ 5 cm high)
- 2 (12-inch/30 cm) round vanilla cakes (2 inches/ 5 cm high)
- 15½ cups (3.875 L) buttercream
- 105 oz. (3 kg) white fondant
- gel food coloring—blue
- cornstarch
- royal icing
- clear piping gel

OVERVIEW

Mosaics are very time-consuming designs. The following may take up to two days for a novice to complete. For more elaborate designs, allot yourself even more time to complete.

- Make the six cakes and set aside to cool (approx. 3 hrs.)

- Level, split, fill, and assemble the tiers (1 hr.)

- Cover each tier with buttercream (1½ hrs., including refrigeration)

- Cover the tiers with fondant and assemble (1 hr.)

- Draw a design of your choice on the side of the cake (10 mins.)

- Cut and attach the fondant tiles (for this design, approx. 2½ hrs.)

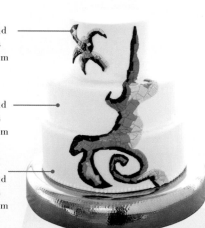

two 6-inch (15 cm) round vanilla cakes (2 inches/5 cm high)

two 10-inch (25 cm) round vanilla cakes (2 inches/5 cm high)

two 12-inch (30 cm) round vanilla cakes (2 inches/5 cm high)

STEP 1

Level the tops of the cakes, split the cakes in half horizontally, and fill them with buttercream. Place each on its corresponding cake board to make three tiers, each 4 inches (10 cm) high.

STEP 2

Cover the tiers with a thin layer of buttercream. Chill until firm. Cover with a second coat of buttercream and smooth with a dough scraper. Refrigerate for 1 hour.

STEP 3

Color 1 ounce (28 g) of fondant a deep royal blue, 1 ounce (28 g) a medium sky blue, and 1 ounce (28 g) a light blue. Set aside, covered with plastic wrap.

STEP 4

Roll out the remaining white fondant to ¼ inch (6 mm) thick and cover the 6-inch (15 cm) round tier. Smooth with the fondant smoother and trim excess with the pizza cutter. Repeat with the remaining tiers.

STEP 5

Cut dowels into eighteen 4-inch (10 cm) long pieces. Leave one dowel 12 inches (30 cm) long, and sharpen one end. Insert 10 dowels vertically into the 12-inch (30 cm) tier and eight into the 10-inch (25 cm) tier. Space them evenly. Stack the 10-inch (25 cm) tier on top of the 12-inch (30 cm) tier and the 6-inch (15 cm) on top of the 10-inch (25 cm) tier. Drive the 12-inch (30 cm) dowel vertically through the center of all three tiers. Cover the hole on top with a dab of royal icing.

STEP 6

With the edible ink pen, draw a design of your choice on one side of the cake, from top to bottom.

STEP 7

Roll out the royal blue fondant to ⅛ inch (3 mm) thick, and then cut out small square tiles with the cutter. Attach the tiles with water to the left-hand side of the design you outlined. Use the utility knife to trim the tiles to follow the curve of the design.

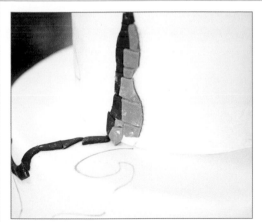

STEP 8

Roll out the sky-blue fondant to ⅛ inch (3 mm) thick. Cut out square tiles and attach with a little water to the design you outlined, as close as possible to the line of royal-blue tiles and leaving space on the right-hand side of the design for the light blue tiles. Trim the tiles with the utility knife, as needed, to make them fit.

STEP 9

Roll out the light blue fondant to ⅛ inch (3 mm) thick. Cut out square tiles and attach with a little water to fill out the design. Trim tiles to make them follow the contour of the design.

STEP 10

Paint over the tiles with clear piping gel to create a glazed tile effect. Put the cake on a cake stand.

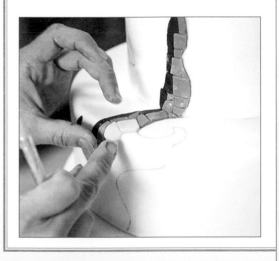

BAROQUE

The damask print has been popular since the early Middle Ages.
The print is becoming popular again, and today it can be seen in modern
interior designs and at many weddings.

TOOLS

- large pastry brush
- 16-inch (40 cm) round cake drum
- rolling pin
- sharp knife
- 4-inch (10 cm) square cake board
- 6-inch (15 cm) round cake board
- 8-inch (20 cm) square cake board
- 12-inch (30 cm) round cake board
- 14-inch (35 cm) square cake board
- serrated knife
- large and small offset spatulas
- dough scraper
- fondant smoother
- pizza cutter
- plastic wrap
- ruler
- quilting tool
- damask stencil
- dowels and shears
- pencil sharpener
- piping bag and coupler
- #18 piping tip
- fuchsia satin ribbon
- glue stick

MATERIALS

- piping gel
- 220 oz. (6 kg) white fondant
- cornstarch
- 2 (4-inch/10 cm) square vanilla cakes (2 inches/ 5 cm high)
- 2 (6-inch/15 cm) round vanilla cakes (2 inches/ 5 cm high)
- 2 (8-inch/20 cm) square vanilla cakes (2 inches/ 5 cm high)
- 2 (12-inch/30 cm) round vanilla cakes (2 inches/ 5 cm high)
- 2 (14-inch/35 cm) square vanilla cakes (2 inches/ 5 cm high)
- 28 cups (7 L) buttercream
- petal dust—black, fuchsia
- royal icing

OVERVIEW

This cake will require two days to complete.

DAY ONE
- Cover the cake drum with fondant (½ hr.)
- Make the 10 cakes and set aside to cool (approx. 5 hrs.)

DAY TWO
- Level, split, fill, and assemble the tiers (2 hrs.)
- Cover each tier with buttercream (2½ hrs., including refrigeration)
- Cover the tiers with fondant (2 hrs.)
- Use the quilting tool to decorate the tiers covered with black fondant (1 hr.)
- Apply the stencil to the tiers covered with white fondant (approx. 1 hr., allow 3 hrs for drying)
- Assemble all the tiers (1 hr.)
- Final touches (45 mins.)

two 4-inch (10 cm) square vanilla cakes (2 inches/5 cm high)

two 6-inch (15 cm) round vanilla cakes (2 inches/5 cm high)

two 8-inch (20 cm) square vanilla cakes (2 inches/5 cm high)

two 12-inch (30 cm) round vanilla cakes (2 inches/5 cm high)

two 14-inch (35 cm) square vanilla cakes (2 inches/5 cm high)

STEP 1

Spread piping gel evenly over the cake drum with the pastry brush. Roll out 10 ounces (280 g) of the white fondant to ¼ inch (6 mm) thick and cover the cake drum. Trim the excess.

STEP 2

With each cake layer on its corresponding cake board, level the tops of all five tiers, split the cakes in half horizontally, and fill between the layers with buttercream. Cover each tier with a thin layer of buttercream and refrigerate for 20 minutes. Cover the top and sides with a thicker coat of buttercream, smooth with the dough scraper, and refrigerate for 1 hour.

STEP 3

Dye 150 ounces (4 kg) of the white fondant with the black petal dust. Roll out to ¼ inch (6 mm) thick and cover the 4-inch (10 cm), 8-inch (20 cm), and 14-inch (35 cm) square tiers. Smooth with the fondant smoother and trim excess with the pizza cutter. Cover the tiers with plastic wrap to prevent the fondant from drying out.

STEP 4

Beginning with the 4-inch (10 cm) tier, place the ruler along the base of the cake and mark it at 1-inch (2.5 cm) intervals with a small knife. Mark it at the same 1-inch (2.5 cm) intervals along the top of the tier. Repeat on all sides.

STEP 5

Holding the ruler vertically, line up the first mark on the bottom with the third mark on the top. Using the quilting tool, make a diagonal line joining these two points. Continue using the ruler and the quilting tool to join the second mark on the bottom to the fourth mark on the top. Continue until there are no more marks on the top. Then, begin joining the first mark on the top with the third mark on the bottom. Repeating this will reveal a quilted diamond pattern. Repeat this procedure on all the square tiers, covered with black fondant.

STEP 6

Roll out the remaining white fondant to ¼ inch (6 mm) thick and cover the 6-inch (15 cm) and 12-inch (30 cm) round tiers. Smooth with the fondant smoother and trim the excess with the pizza cutter.

STEP 7

Dye ½ cup (125 ml) of royal icing with black petal dust. Hold the damask stencil against the side of the 6-inch (15 cm) round tier (you may need someone to help you hold it steady).

STEP 8

Using a small offset spatula, spread a thin layer of black royal icing on the stencil. Scrape off the excess.

STEP 9

Gently lift off the stencil, without smudging the design. Repeat this procedure until the entire side of the cake is covered with the damask print. Do the same for the 12-inch (30 cm) round tier. Allow to dry for 3 hours.

STEP 10

Cut the dowels into twenty-six 4-inch (10 cm) long pieces. Insert eight vertically into the 14-inch (35 cm) tier, eight into the 12-inch (30 cm) tier, six into the 8-inch (20 cm) tier, and four into the 6-inch (15 cm) tier. Space the dowels evenly and leave a space of 2 inches (5 cm) from the edge. Transfer the 14-inch (35 cm) tier to the cake drum, securing it with a dab of royal icing. Place a dab of royal icing on the top of the dowels and begin stacking the tiers: the 12-inch (30 cm) tier on top of the 14-inch (35 cm) tier, the 8-inch (20 cm) on the 12-inch (30 cm), the 6-inch (15 cm) on the 8-inch (20 cm), and the 4-inch (10 cm) tier on the 6-inch (15 cm). Sharpen one end of a 12-inch (30 cm) long dowel. Drive it vertically through the center of the tiers. Cover the hole on top of the 4-inch (10 cm) tier with some royal icing.

STEP 11
Dye ½ cup (125 ml) of royal icing with fuchsia petal dust. Fill the piping bag and, using the #18 piping tip, pipe a border along the bottom of all five tiers.

STEP 12
Attach the fuchsia ribbon to the cake drum with the glue stick. Tie a small bow and attach the bow to the front of the cake drum with more glue.

BABY SHOWER

The birth of a baby is always a special occasion. Celebrate with this cute design. Change the colors, if you want, for a baby girl shower. Start this cake at least a day in advance to let the fondant decorations dry.

TOOLS

- pastry brush
- 14-inch (35 cm) square cake drum
- rolling pin
- sharp knife
- serrated knife
- offset spatula
- 5-inch (13 cm) square cake board
- 7-inch (18 cm) square cake board
- 8-inch (20 cm) square cake board
- 9-inch (23 cm) square cake board
- dough scraper
- fondant smoother
- pizza cutter
- plastic wrap
- fondant ribbon cutter
- paintbrush
- small circle cutter
- scissors
- ruler
- small blossom cutter
- #12 piping tip
- dowels and shears
- pencil sharpener
- piping bag and coupler
- large and medium scalloped cutters
- blue satin ribbon
- glue stick

MATERIALS

- piping gel
- 160 oz. (4.5 kg) ivory fondant
- cornstarch
- 2 (5-inch/13 cm) square vanilla cakes (2 inches/ 5 cm high)
- 2 (7-inch/18 cm) square vanilla cakes (2 inches/ 5 cm high)
- 2 (8-inch/20 cm) square vanilla cakes (2 inches/ 5 cm high)
- 2 (9-inch/23 cm) square vanilla cakes (2 inches/ 5 cm high)
- 14 cups (3.5 L) buttercream
- gel food coloring—green, blue
- royal icing

OVERVIEW

This cake will require two days to complete.

DAY ONE
- Cover cake drum with fondant (15 mins.)
- Prepare fondant bows (1½ hrs.) (see steps 11–14)

DAY TWO
- Make the eight cakes and set aside to cool (approx. 4 hrs.)
- Level, split, fill, and assemble the tiers (2 hrs.)
- Cover each tier with buttercream (2½ hrs., including refrigeration)
- Cover the tiers with fondant (2 hrs.)
- Decorate each tier (2½ hrs.)
- Assemble all the tiers (1 hr.)
- Final touches (½ hr.)

two 5-inch (13 cm) square vanilla cakes (2 inches/5 cm high)

two 7-inch (18 cm) square vanilla cakes (2 inches/5 cm high)

two 8-inch (20 cm) square vanilla cakes (2 inches/5 cm high)

two 9-inch (23 cm) square vanilla cakes (2 inches/5 cm high)

STEP 1

With the pastry brush, spread piping gel over the 14-inch (35 cm) cake drum. On a cornstarch-covered work surface, roll out 10 ounces (280 g) of ivory fondant to ¼ inch (6 mm) thick. Cover the cake drum and trim off the excess with the sharp knife.

STEP 2

Level the tops of all the cakes with the serrated knife. Split them in half horizontally. Place each cake on its corresponding cake board, and fill all four layers with buttercream. Cover the tiers with a thin layer of buttercream. Chill until firm. Cover with a second coat of buttercream and smooth with the dough scraper. Refrigerate for 1 hour.

STEP 3

Dye 80 ounces (2.3 kg) of fondant pastel blue and 4 ounces (113 g) pastel green. Roll out the remaining ivory fondant to ¼ inch (6 mm) thick and cover the 5-inch (13 cm) tier. Smooth with the fondant smoother. Trim off excess. Save trimmings, and wrap in plastic wrap. Repeat with the 8-inch (20 cm) tier.

STEP 4

Roll out the blue fondant to ¼ inch (6 mm) thick and cover the 7-inch (18 cm) tier. Smooth with the fondant smoother. Trim off excess and save trimmings, wrapping them in plastic wrap. Repeat with the 9-inch (23 cm) tier.

STEP 5

Transfer the 9-inch (23 cm) tier to the prepared cake drum. Roll out the green fondant to ⅛ inch (3 mm) thick. With the fondant ribbon cutter, cut out strips, each 1½ inches (4 cm) wide. Roll up the strips to keep them from drying out while you work. Starting ¼ inch (6 mm) from the edge, attach three green strips vertically on each side of the 9-inch (23 cm) tier. Space them evenly on each side.

STEP 6

Now roll out the reserved ivory fondant to
⅛ inch (3 mm) thick and cut out ¼-inch (6 mm)
wide strips. Using a wet paintbrush, attach these
along both sides of each green strip. Trim off
the excess fondant along the top of the tier.

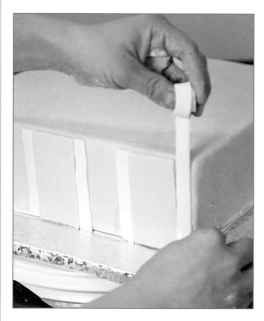

STEP 7

Roll out the reserved blue and green fondants
to ⅛ inch (3 mm) thick. With the small circle
cutter, cut out small round dots from each
fondant color. Attach the dots to the sides of
the ivory-colored 8-inch (20 cm) tier, alternating
the colors.

STEP 8

Now decorate the 7-inch (18 cm) tier. Roll
out the rest of the green fondant to ⅛ inch
(3 mm) thick. Cut out four strips, each ½ inch
(1 cm) wide and 9 inches (23 cm) long. Attach
a strip along the bottom edge of each side
of the 7-inch (18 cm) tier. Pinch together
where the strips meet at the corners and cut
off the excess with scissors.

STEP 9

With the ruler, mark a line 2 inches (5 cm) from the top of the tier. Roll out ivory fondant to ¼ inch (6 mm) thick. Cut four strips that are ½ inch (1 cm) wide and 9 inches (23 cm) long each. Attach them to the marked line on the cake. Pinch together where the strips meet at the corners and cut with scissors.

  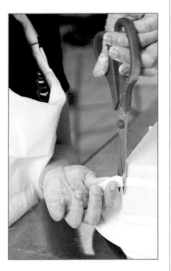

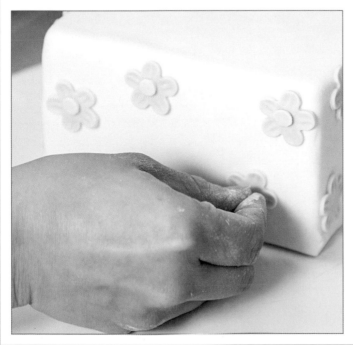

STEP 10

To decorate the 5-inch (13 cm) tier, roll out the remaining blue fondant to ⅛ inch (3 mm) thick. Cut out flowers with the blossom cutter. Attach the flowers to the 5-inch (13 cm) tier. Roll out green fondant to ⅛ inch (3 mm) thick and cut out dots with the #12 tip. Attach the dots to the center of each flower.

STEP 11

Tear off pieces of plastic wrap and roll them into balls.

STEP 12

Roll out the remaining ivory fondant to ⅛ inch (3 mm) thick. Cut out four strips that are 2 inches (5 cm) wide and 8 inches (20 cm) long. Cut four more strips, 2 inches (5 cm) wide and 3 inches (8 cm) long. Wet the center of one 8-inch (20 cm) long strip. Place a piece of balled-up plastic wrap on each side of the wet spot.

STEP 13

Bring both ends of the strip toward the wet center of the strip. Pinch together.

STEP 14

Wet a 3-inch (8 cm) strip and wrap it around the center of the bow. Set aside to dry overnight. Repeat with the other strips, making a total of four bows.

STEP 15

Cut twenty 4-inch (10 cm) long dowels and one 12-inch (30 cm) long dowel. Sharpen one end of the 12-inch (30 cm) dowel. Insert eight dowels vertically into the 9-inch (23 cm) tier, six into the 8-inch (20 cm) tier, and six into the 7-inch (18 cm) tier. Stack one tier on top of the other, placing the 9-inch (23 cm) tier on the bottom, then the 8-inch (20 cm) tier, then the 7-inch (18 cm) tier, and ending with the 5-inch (13 cm) tier. Turn the tiers so they are staggered, instead of having the edges parallel to each other. This will leave the corners of the 9-inch (23 cm) tier open for the bows. Insert the 12-inch (30 cm) long dowel through the center of the tiers. Pipe white beads of royal icing along the base of each tier.

STEP 16

Roll out blue fondant to ⅛ inch (3 mm) thick. Cut out a scalloped circle with the large scalloped cutter. Attach with a little water to the top of the 5-inch (13 cm) tier. Roll out the green fondant and cut out a circle with the medium scalloped cutter. Moisten and attach to the center of the blue circle.

STEP 17

On each corner of the 9-inch (23 cm) tier, attach a strip of ivory fondant that is 2 inches (5 cm) wide and 6 inches (15 cm) long. Cut out a "V" shape from each end. With royal icing, attach the fondant bows on each strip. Remove the plastic wrap. Attach the satin ribbon to the cake drum with the glue stick.

TOPSY-TURVY

Who can resist the look of a whimsical cake? The silver and gold colors complement each other and contrast beautifully with the black background—all topped with a golden crown. The crown will need to dry overnight, so plan ahead.

TOOLS

- large and small serrated knives
- offset spatula
- 12-inch (30 cm) round cake board
- 6-inch (15 cm) round cake board
- dough scraper
- rolling pin
- fondant smoother
- pizza cutter
- small sharp knife
- plastic wrap
- medium quilting tool
- paintbrushes
- painter's palette
- fondant ribbon cutter
- heart-shaped cutter
- 4-inch (10 cm) round pan
- scissors
- cake stand

MATERIALS

- 2 (8-inch/20 cm) round vanilla cakes (2 inches/ 5 cm high)
- 3½ cups (875 ml) buttercream
- 30 oz. (850 g) white fondant
- gel food coloring—black, golden yellow
- cornstarch
- luster dust or edible glitter—gold, silver
- vodka
- black Candy Melts

OVERVIEW

This cake will require two days to complete.

DAY ONE
- Make the yellow fondant crown (1 hr.) (See step 12)

DAY TWO
- Make the two cakes and set aside to cool (approx. 1 hr.)
- Level, split, fill, and assemble the two tiers (½ hr.)
- Cut and shape the cake (approx. 1 hr.)

- Cover the cake with buttercream (1½ hrs., including refrigeration)
- Cover the cake with fondant (1 hr.)
- Decorate the cake with the quilting tool (½ hr.)
- Cut out and attach the diamond fondant pieces and balls (1 hr.)
- Final touches (1 hr.)

two 8-inch (20 cm) round vanilla cakes (2 inches/5 cm high)

STEP 1

With the large serrated knife, level the cake layers, split them in half horizontally, and fill with buttercream. With the cake on the 12-inch (30 cm) cake board, refrigerate for 1 hour to firm up the cake. Spread a dab of buttercream on the top of the cake and place the 6-inch (15 cm) cake board in the center. This will become the bottom of the cake.

STEP 2

With a small serrated knife, carve around the top edge of the cake, using the 6-inch (15 cm) board as the guide.

STEP 3

With a downward motion, cut the cake from the 6-inch (15 cm) diameter on top to the 8-inch (20 cm) diameter on the bottom. This will give the cake tapered sides.

STEP 4

Flip the cake upside down and, holding the large serrated knife at a 45-degree angle against the side of the cake, cut straight across to cut a wedge off the top.

STEP 5

Spread a little buttercream on the top of the cake that remains. Turn the wedge 180 degrees and place it back on the top of the cake. Now the cake will have a tapered top and tapered sides.

STEP 6

Spread a thin coat of buttercream on the top and sides of the cake. Refrigerate until firm. Cover the top and sides with a thicker coat of buttercream. Smooth with a dough scraper and refrigerate for 1 hour. Color 24 ounces (680 g) of fondant black. Roll out to ¼ inch (6 mm) thick and cover the cake.

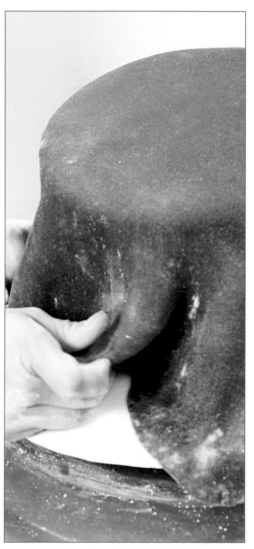

STEP 7

Smooth with the fondant smoother, and trim off excess with the pizza cutter. Save the excess black fondant, and cover it with plastic wrap. Press the quilting tool into the sides of the cake. The markings will act as a guide to where the gold and silver diamonds will be placed.

STEP 9

Wet each diamond with a little water and attach them to the side of the cake. Vertically, alternate between yellow and gray. Leave the next row of diamonds black. Then, repeat with the yellow and gray diamonds. Some may need to be cut (use the small sharp knife).

STEP 8

Dye 2 ounces (56 g) of fondant gray and 4 ounces (113 g) golden yellow. Roll out the gray fondant to ⅛ inch (3 mm) thick. With the quilting tool, cut out diamond shapes. Repeat with the yellow fondant. Save the excess fondant, wrapped in plastic wrap.

STEP 10

Roll out ½-teaspoon (2 ml) balls with the leftover yellow and gray fondant. Roll out ¼-teaspoon (1 ml) balls with the black fondant. Attach the balls to the base of the cake with a little water, alternating the colors.

STEP 11

Mix the gold luster dust or edible glitter with vodka on the painter's palette. Do the same with the silver luster dust or edible glitter. With a small paintbrush, paint the yellow diamonds and balls gold. Then, paint the gray diamonds and balls silver.

STEP 12

Roll out the remaining yellow fondant to ¼ inch (6 mm) thick. With the fondant ribbon cutter, cut out a strip that is 5 inches (13 cm) wide and 15 inches (38 cm) long. Using the bottom half of a heart-shaped cutter, cut pieces from one long side of the strip to make pointy ends. Wrap this strip around a 4-inch (10 cm) round pan. Cut off the excess with scissors and pinch the ends together. This will be the crown. Let dry overnight. When it has dried, remove the pan. Paint the crown gold with the paintbrush. Roll out six ¼-teaspoon (1 ml) balls of gray fondant. Attach them to each of the pointed ends of the crown and paint them silver. Attach the crown to the top of the cake with some melted black Candy Melts. Transfer the cake to the round cake stand.

FANCY CUSHION

The look of your favorite cushion can be easily replicated in a cake.
The gilded buttons and tassels make it extra fancy.

TOOLS

- 14-inch (35 cm) square cake board
- serrated knife
- offset spatula
- dough scraper
- rolling pin
- fondant smoother
- plastic wrap
- pizza cutter
- small sharp knife
- dog bone tool
- veining tool
- floral mold
- clay gun with rope attachment
- utility knife
- paintbrushes
- clothing steamer
- cake stand

MATERIALS

- 1 (8-inch/20 cm) square chocolate cake (3 inches/ 8 cm high)
- 3 cups (750 ml) buttercream
- 38 oz. (1 kg) white fondant
- gel food coloring—red, lemon yellow, leaf green
- cornstarch
- royal icing
- brown petal dust
- luster dust or edible glitter—gold
- vodka

OVERVIEW

This cake will require two days to complete.

DAY ONE
- Make the cake and set aside to cool (approx. 1 hr.)
- Level, split, fill, and assemble (1 hr.)

You can split and fill the cake on day one and then put it in the freezer. Freezing the cake will make it easier to carve. In this case, you will assemble the cake on day two.

DAY TWO
- Cut and shape the cake (approx. 1 hr.)

- Cover with buttercream (1½ hrs., including refrigeration)

- Cover with fondant (1 hr.)

- Make the top of the cushion and decorate it with the fondant buttons (1 hr.)

- Prepare and attach the fondant rope and tassels (1 hr.)

- Final touches (½ hr.)

One 8-inch (20 cm) round chocolate cake (3 inches/ 8 cm high)

STEP 1

On the 14-inch (35 cm) board, level the top of the 8-inch (20 cm) square cake with the serrated knife. Split horizontally into three layers. Fill between the layers with buttercream and chill for 1 hour, or freeze overnight, to firm up the cake.

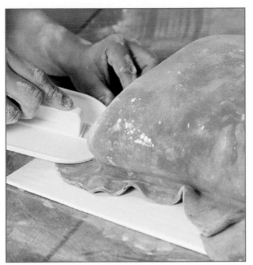

STEP 2

With the serrated knife, round out the edges of the cake, carving until the edges are more sloped down at the top and the middle is more raised, to simulate a cushion. Cover with a light coating of buttercream. Chill until firm. Cover with a second, thicker coat of buttercream and smooth with the dough scraper. Refrigerate for 1 hour.

STEP 3

Dye 36 ounces (945 g) of white fondant with red, yellow, and a touch of green food colorings to achieve a burnt-orange color. On a cornstarch-covered surface, roll fondant out to ¼ inch (6 mm) thick and cover the cushion. Smooth with the fondant smoother and trim off the excess.

STEP 4

Using the sharp knife, push in the fondant at the base of the cake.

STEP 5
Use the dog bone tool to make a dent in the places where the buttons will sit.

STEP 6
With the veining tool, mark lines around the dents to imitate the puckering of fabric.

STEP 7
Dye the remaining 2 ounces (55 g) of white fondant a golden yellow. Roll out ¼-teaspoon (1 ml) balls. Press the balls into the floral mold to flatten and add texture, creating button shapes. Glue each button with a dab of royal icing onto the dented spots on the cushion.

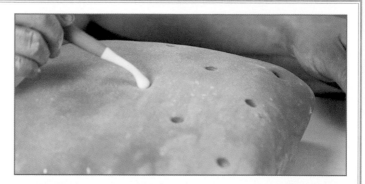

STEP 8

Fill the clay gun with yellow fondant. Squeeze out a long string. Twist the string of fondant to achieve a rope effect. Attach to the cushion with a little water.

STEP 9

Roll out a little of the remaining yellow fondant to 1/16 inch (1.5 mm) thick. Use the utility knife to cut small slits into the fondant.

STEP 10

Moisten the uncut portion of the piece of fondant and roll it up. Make four of these "tassels" and attach them to the corners of the cushion with a little water. Roll out four 1/4-teaspoon (1 ml) balls and attach to the top of the tassel to make the knot of the tassel.

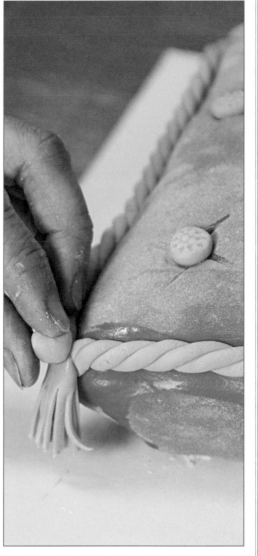

STEP 11

Apply brown petal dust with a paintbrush to the "puckered" lines around the buttons of the cushion. Then, mix the gold luster dust or edible glitter with vodka and paint the rope, tassels, and buttons of the cushion gold.

STEP 12

With the clothing steamer, steam the entire cake to remove the cornstarch. Transfer the cake to a cake stand.

ROSE BOUQUET

Gum paste flowers can be quite time-consuming to make, especially for the novice. Starting one week in advance is always a good idea. When your guests are stunned by the lifelike beauty of this bouquet, it will all seem worth it.

TOOLS

- pastry brush
- 10-inch (25 cm) round cake drum
- small rolling pin
- small palette knife
- toothpicks
- styrofoam block
- small, medium, and large rose cutters
- plastic wrap
- piece of thin foam
- utility knife
- rounded stick
- calyx cutter
- serrated knife
- offset spatula
- dough scraper
- pizza cutter
- sugar-craft gun and large circle disk
- small paintbrush
- ¾-inch (2 cm) wide red and white satin ribbons
- glue stick

MATERIALS

- 88 oz. (2.5 kg) fondant
- gel food coloring—red, leaf green, brown, lemon yellow, ivory
- piping gel
- vodka
- 18 oz. (510 g) gum paste
- shortening
- 2 (6-inch/15 cm) round chocolate cakes (3 inches/ 8 cm high)
- 4 cups (1 L) buttercream
- cornstarch
- royal icing

OVERVIEW

Gum paste flowers can be very labor intensive. In order to complete enough roses to cover the entire cake, we recommend that the roses be made over the span of a week.

DAY ONE
- Prepare the cake drum and cover with fondant (15 mins.)

DAY TWO
- Make the cakes and set aside to cool (approx. 1 hr.)

- Level, split, fill, and assemble each tier (1 hr.)

- Cover the cake with buttercream (1½ hrs., including refrigeration)

- Cover cake with fondant (½ hr.)

- Prepare and attach the fondant stems (1 hr.)

- Attach the previously prepared fondant roses (1½ hrs.)

two 6-inch (15 cm) round chocolate cakes (3 inches/8 cm high)

STEP 1

Divide 18 ounces (510 g) of fondant into three balls. Color the balls dark brown, medium brown, and light brown. Roll each ball into a sausage shape. Twist the three colors together and mix them just enough to achieve a marbled effect.

STEP 2

With the pastry brush, brush the piping gel onto the cake drum. With the rolling pin, roll out the marbled brown fondant and cover the cake drum. Using a small palette knife, score the fondant to get a wood-grain effect. Dilute the ivory gel color with some vodka and brush it over the fondant-covered cake drum to stain it.

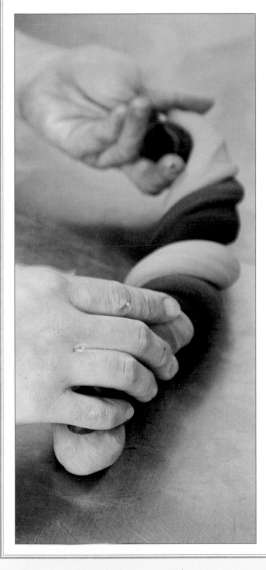

STEP 3

Color 16 ounces (453 g) of the gum paste a deep red and color 2 ounces (56 g) green. Break off pieces of the red gum paste and roll into ½-, ¼-, and ⅛-teaspoon (2 ml, 1 ml, and 0.5 ml) balls. You will need a total of 60 balls. Roll each ball into a teardrop shape. Stick a toothpick into the wide end of each teardrop, and then stick them upright into the styrofoam. Allow to dry overnight.

Take the second set of petals. With the rounded stick, thin out the edges of all the petals on the piece of thin foam. Make incisions with the utility knife to separate the petals a little.

STEP 4
The next day, with the rolling pin, roll out the remaining red gum paste as thinly as possible on a surface greased with shortening. Cut out four sets of petals with the large rose cutter. Place one set on the thin piece of foam and cover the other three sets with plastic wrap. Using the utility knife, cut out one petal from the first set. Using the rounded stick like a rolling pin, thin the petal on one side.

STEP 5
Lightly moisten the thick side of the petal and wrap it around the teardrop cone with the thin side of the cone up. Discard the other petals on the set.

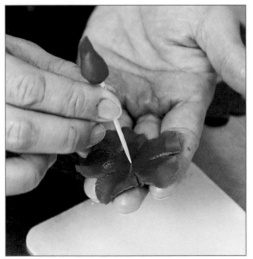

STEP 7
Wet the center of the petal set and insert the toothpick with the teardrop cone into the center. Move the petals up the toothpick until the petals reach the base of the cone.

STEP 8

Attach the petals to the cone one by one, alternating with the petals that are opposite each other.

STEP 9

Repeat with the remaining two sets of petals until you have a full rose. Furl the petals gently with your fingers to get a natural look.

STEP 10

Roll out the green gum paste thinly. Cut it with the calyx cutter. Working on the piece of foam and using the rounded stick, elongate the points of the gum-paste calyx. Wet the center with a little water and attach to the base of the rose. Stand the rose back in the styrofoam to dry. Repeat all the steps with the small, medium, and large rose cutters. You will need at least 60 roses to cover the cake.

ASSEMBLING THE BOUQUET

STEP 11

Level the top of one of the cake layers with a serrated knife and leave the second layer with a rounded top. Split both layers in half horizontally with the serrated knife. Stack the layers, starting with the leveled layer and ending with the rounded top of the second layer on top. Fill between each layer with ¼ cup (60 ml) of buttercream, spreading it using the offset spatula. Cover the top and sides of the cake tower with a thin, smooth coating of buttercream. Refrigerate until firm, then apply second coat of buttercream, and smooth with a dough scraper. Refrigerate for 1 hour, until firm.

STEP 12

Color 52 ounces (1.5 kg) of the fondant dark green. With the yellow and green gel colors, dye 18 ounces (510 g) of the fondant a light shade of green.

STEP 13

Roll out 28 ounces (793 g) of the dark green fondant to ¼ inch (6 mm) thick on a surface dusted with cornstarch. Cover the prepared cake with it and trim off the excess with the pizza cutter. Save the trimmings and cover with plastic wrap. Transfer the covered cake to the cake drum. Secure with a dab of royal icing.

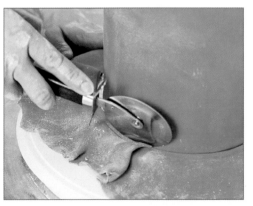

STEP 14

Soften the dark green and light green fondant with shortening. Using the sugar-craft gun and circle disk, squeeze out 4-inch (10 cm) long rose stems with the dark green and light green fondant. You will need about 50 stems of each color to cover the cake. With a paintbrush and water, moisten each stem and attach it to the side of the cake. Alternate between the two shades of green. You may need to trim the tops with the utility knife to keep all the stems even.

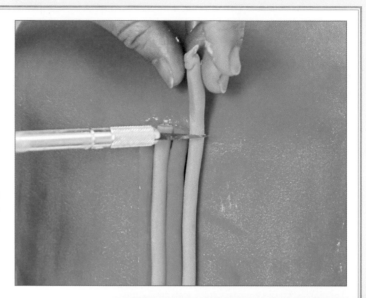

STEP 15

Begin attaching the dried roses to the top of the cake with green-colored royal icing. Start with the large roses and fill any gaps with the medium and small roses.

STEP 16

Use the glue stick to attach the red satin ribbon to the cake drum. Tie the white satin ribbon around the middle of the bouquet.

LUSTROUS PEACOCK

Capturing the beauty of a peacock, this three-tiered cake makes a stunning centerpiece for any celebration. Note the delicacy of each feather and the edible brooch. Give yourself a week to make this cake.

TOOLS

- 14-inch (35 cm) round cake drum
- pastry brush
- rolling pin
- fondant ribbon cutter
- small and large paintbrushes
- parchment paper
- cookie sheet
- small and large oval cutters
- two piping bags and couplers
- #2 piping tip
- pizza cutter
- utility knife
- flower formers
- 4-inch (10 cm) round pan
- 6-inch (15 cm) round pan
- 12-inch (30 cm) square cake drum
- painter's palette
- 6-inch (15 cm) round cake board
- pencil
- scissors
- 9-inch (23 cm) petal-shaped pan
- 10-inch (25 cm) round cake board
- 12-inch (30 cm) round cake board
- serrated knife
- offset spatula
- dough scraper
- fondant smoother
- 14 (4 inch/10 cm long) wooden dowels
- one (12-inch/30 cm long) dowel
- pencil sharpener
- ¾-inch (2 cm) wide purple grosgrain ribbon
- glue stick

MATERIALS

- 135 oz. (3.8 kg) fondant
- gel food coloring—sky blue, violet, black
- 10 oz. (280 g) gum paste
- piping gel
- cornstarch
- luster dust/edible glitter— midnight blue, peacock blue, silver, pearl, deep rose, gold
- royal icing
- silver dragées/fondant beads
- shortening
- vodka
- black petal dust
- pearl dragées/fondant beads
- 2 (6-inch/15 cm) round vanilla cakes (2 inches/ 5 cm high)
- 2 (9-inch/23 cm) petal-shaped vanilla cakes (2 inches/ 5 cm high)
- 2 (12-inch/30 cm) round vanilla cakes (2 inches/ 5 cm high)
- 15 cups (3.75 L) buttercream

OVERVIEW

You should begin preparing this cake one week in advance.

ONE WEEK AHEAD
- Cover the cake drum (15 mins.)
- Make the 12 bow loops (1½ hrs.)
- Prepare the fondant brooch (1 hr.)
- Prepare the hearts and scrolls (2 hrs.)
- Make the black fondant feathers (1½ hrs.)

THREE DAYS AHEAD
- Paint all the hearts, scrolls, and ovals with gold paint (1 hr.)
- Final touches to the fondant

feathers (1 hr.)
- Assemble the bows (1 hr.)

FINAL DAY
- Make the six cakes and set aside to cool (approx. 3 hrs.)
- Level, split, fill, and assemble the tiers (2 hrs.)
- Cover each tier with buttercream (2½ hrs., including refrigeration)
- Cover the tiers with fondant (2 hrs.)
- Assemble all the tiers (1 hr.)
- Final touches (1½ hrs.)

two 6-inch (15 cm) round vanilla cakes (2 inches/5 cm high)

two 9-inch (23 cm) petal-shaped vanilla cakes (2 inches/5 cm high)

two 12-inch (30 cm) round vanilla cakes (2 inches/5 cm high)

ONE WEEK AHEAD

STEP 1

Color 105 ounces (3 kg) fondant sky blue and 25 ounces (708 g) light violet. Color the gum paste black.

STEP 2

Brush the 14-inch (35 cm) round cake drum with piping gel. On a cornstarch-dusted surface, roll out the violet fondant ¼ inch (6 mm) thick and cover the cake drum.

STEP 3

Roll out the remaining violet fondant to ¼ inch (6 mm) thick. With the ribbon cutter, cut out 12 strips that are 2 inches (5 cm) wide and 4 inches (10 cm) long. Set aside any remnants. Flip one strip over. Moisten the outer edges of the strip on both sides. Fold over about ¼ inch (6 mm) on each side so that the strip is now 1½ inches (4 cm) wide.

STEP 4

Place some rolled up plastic wrap in the center of the fondant strip and pinch both ends together. Repeat with the remaining strips to get 12 bow loops. (Remove plastic wrap once the bow loops are dry).

STEP 5

With a small paintbrush, dust the center of each bow loop with the rose luster dust or edible glitter. Place on parchment paper to dry.

STEP 6

Roll out 2 ounces (56 g) of white fondant. With the oval cutters, cut out three large ovals and one small oval. Spread each with a little royal icing thinned with water, and then cover each with fine silver dragées or fondant beads. Set aside to dry.

STEP 7

Fill a piping bag with royal icing and attach the #2 piping tip. Pipe small hearts and curled scrolls about ²/₃ inch (1.5 cm) in size onto parchment paper. You will need enough to cover the base of all three tiers. Make extras in case of breakage. Set aside to dry.

STEP 8

Roll out the black gum paste as thinly as possible on a surface greased with shortening. Using the pizza cutter, cut out feather shapes.

STEP 9

Cut fine slits into both sides of the feathers with a sharp utility knife. You will need seven feathers and a few extras in case of breakage. Place on flower formers to dry.

THREE DAYS AHEAD

STEP 10

Using a 4-inch (10 cm) round pan and a 6-inch (15 cm) round pan, trace and cut out circles from the 12-inch (30 cm) square cake drum. Brush both with piping gel and cover them with the sky-blue fondant. These will be the separators for the cake tiers.

STEP 11

Make gold paint by mixing gold luster dust or edible glitter and vodka. Paint all the hearts, scrolls, and ovals gold. Let dry. Attach scrolls to the ovals using royal icing to form gold brooches.

STEP 12

Gently dust the feathers with black petal dust.

STEP 13

Tint a small amount of royal icing black, and pipe a line lengthwise down each feather with the #2 piping tip. Let dry.

STEP 14

Roll three ¼-teaspoon (1 ml) balls of violet fondant. Gently push four bow loops into each ball to form a bow. Place a dab of royal icing in the center and attach a large gold brooch to cover the fondant-ball center. Adorn each brooch with a few pearl dragées or fondant beads.

ASSEMBLING THE CAKE

STEP 15

Level the tops of the cake layers. Split the 6-inch (15 cm) round layers in half horizontally and fill between the layers with buttercream. Set the 6-inch (15 cm) tier on the 6-inch (15 cm) round cake board to make a 4-inch (10 cm) high cake tower.

STEP 16

Using the 9-inch (23 cm) petal pan, trace and cut out a 9-inch (23 cm) petal-shaped cake board from the 10-inch (25 cm) round cake board. Split, fill, and stack the petal-shaped cake layers on this board.

STEP 17

Split, fill, and stack the 12-inch (30 cm) cake layers on the 12-inch (30 cm) round cake board. Cover the cake tiers with buttercream and smooth with the dough scraper. Refrigerate until firm. Cover with a second coat of buttercream and smooth with the dough scraper. Refrigerate for 1 hour.

STEP 18

Roll out the sky-blue fondant to ¼-inch (6 mm) thick. Cover all three tiers and smooth with the fondant smoother. Trim excess fondant with the pizza cutter.

STEP 19

Transfer the 12-inch (30 cm) round cake to the decorated 14-inch (35 cm) cake drum. Secure with a dab of royal icing. Place the 6-inch (15 cm) separator in the center of this tier. Gently trace around the edges of the separator with a knife so you can see where to place the dowels. Remove the separator and insert eight dowels evenly into the area where you have scored. Apply small dabs of royal icing to the tops of each dowel. Place the 6-inch (15 cm) separator back on the tier. Squeeze a dab of royal icing onto the separator. Stack the petal-shaped tier onto the separator. Place the 4-inch (10 cm) separator onto the center of this tier. Score gently, remove the separator, and insert the remaining six dowels evenly into the cake. Place dabs of royal icing on the tops of each dowel. Place the 4-inch (10 cm) separator back onto the cake. Apply a dab of royal icing and place the top tier onto the cake.

STEP 20

Sharpen one end of the 12-inch (30 cm) dowel with the pencil sharpener. Drive the dowel, sharp end down, through the three tiers and the separators. Cover the hole with a dab of royal icing.

STEP 21

With a paintbrush, apply midnight-blue luster dust or edible glitter into the grooves of the petal-shaped tier. Dust peacock-blue luster dust on the edges of all three tiers. With the large paintbrush, dust the tiers with silver and pearl dust.

STEP 22

With small dabs of royal icing, attach the gold hearts along the base of the three tiers. The hearts should be pointing down on the top two tiers and pointing up on the bottom tier.

STEP 23

Randomly attach the violet bows with royal icing, one per tier. Surround each bow with black feathers. Secure with royal icing. Cover the hole on the top tier with the remaining small gold brooch. Attach random pearl dragées or fondant beads to the three tiers. With the glue stick, attach the purple ribbon to the cake drum.

URBAN SAFARI

Bring the look of the jungle to your city life. The unusual shape of the four tiers makes this cake very unique. With its mix of round and square tiers and different prints, this is not your typical wedding cake.

TOOLS

- serrated knife
- offset spatula
- 4-inch (10 cm) square cake board
- dough scraper
- 10-inch (25 cm) square cake board
- 4-inch (10 cm) round cake board
- scissors
- 6-inch (15 cm) round cake board
- 12-inch (30 cm) square cake board
- rolling pin
- fondant smoother
- pizza cutter
- plastic wrap
- dowels and shears
- pencil sharpener
- veining tool
- paintbrush
- painter's palette
- piping bag and coupler
- #12 piping tip
- 16-inch (40 cm) cake drum

MATERIALS

- 2 (4-inch/10 cm) round vanilla cakes (2 inches/ 5 cm high)
- 2 (6-inch/15 cm) square vanilla cakes (2 inches/ 5 cm high)
- 2 (8-inch/20 cm) round vanilla cakes (2 inches/ 5 cm high)
- 2 (12-inch/30 cm) square vanilla cakes (2 inches/ 5 cm high)
- 14½ cups (3.625 L) buttercream
- 135 oz. (3.8 kg) white fondant
- cornstarch
- gel food coloring—black, brown
- vodka
- royal icing

OVERVIEW

This cake will require two days to complete. You can split, fill, and freeze the cake tiers one day in advance to make carving easier.

DAY ONE
- Make the eight cakes and set aside to cool (approx. 4 hrs.)

- Level, split, fill, and assemble each tier (1 hr.)

- Freeze cakes overnight. (This is optional.)

DAY TWO
- Cut and shape each tier (approx. 2 hrs.)

- Cover each tier with buttercream (2 hrs., including refrigeration)

- Cut holes in the top of the bottom three tiers (½ hr.)

- Cover each tier with fondant (1 hr.)

- Assemble the tiers (½ hr.)

- Decorate each tier (2 hrs.)

- Final touches (½ hr.)

two 4-inch (10 cm) round vanilla cakes (2 inches/5 cm high)

two 6-inch (15 cm) square vanilla cakes (2 inches/5 cm high)

two 8-inch (20 cm) round vanilla cakes (2 inches/5 cm high)

two 12-inch (30 cm) square vanilla cakes (2 inches/5 cm high)

STEP 1

Level the tops of all cakes with the serrated knife. Spread buttercream between each pair of cakes of the same size. Chill the four tiers for 1 hour to firm up the cake.

STEP 2

Starting with the 6-inch (15 cm) square tier, spread a dab of buttercream on the top of the cake. Place the 4-inch (10 cm) square cake board on top. With the serrated knife, carve around the top edge of the cake, using the 4-inch (10 cm) board as a guide and sloping down to the 6-inch (15 cm) base.

STEP 3

Flip the cake upside down, keeping the 4-inch (10 cm) board on the bottom of the cake. From the 6-inch- (15 cm) diameter top and, with the serrated knife at a 45-degree angle against the side of the cake, cut straight across to cut a wedge off the top.

STEP 4

Spread some buttercream on the top and put the wedge back on top of the tier, turning it 180 degrees. Cover the entire cake with buttercream and smooth with the dough scraper. Return to the refrigerator for 1 hour.

STEP 5
Repeat steps 2 to 4 with the 12-inch (30 cm) square tier and the 10-inch (25 cm) square board.

STEP 6
Trace a 2-inch (5 cm) circle on the 4-inch (10 cm) round board (this is done as cake boards are usually 4-inches or bigger). Cut out the circle with scissors. Attach the circle to the top of the 4-inch (10 cm) round tier with a dab  of buttercream. Using the board as a guide, carve around the top edge of the cake and slope down toward the 4-inch (10 cm) base.

STEP 7
Flip the cake upside down, keeping the board attached. Hold the knife at a 45-degree angle against the side of the cake and cut straight across to take a wedge off the top.

STEP 8
Turn the wedge around 180 degrees and attach it to the top of the cake with buttercream. Cover the entire cake with buttercream and smooth with the dough scraper. Chill for 1 hour.

STEP 9
Repeat steps 6 to 8 with the 8-inch (20 cm) round tier and the 6-inch (15 cm) round board.

STEP 10

Using the 6-inch (15 cm) round board as a guide, trace a 6-inch (15 cm) circle in the center of the top of the already carved 12-inch (30 cm) square tier (see step 5).

STEP 11

Cut out the circle, down through the entire layer, and remove the circle of cake. The 8-inch (20 cm) round tier will have been carved to taper into a 6-inch (15 cm) round base that will sit in this hole, see step 9. Repeat this process with the 8-inch (20 cm) round tier and 4-inch square board and the 6-inch (15 cm) square tier and 2-inch (5 cm) round board.

STEP 12

Roll out 15 ounces (425 g) of white fondant to ¼-inch (6-mm) thick and cover the tapered 4-inch (10 cm) round tier. Smooth with the fondant smoother, and trim off excess with the pizza cutter, wrapping the trimmings with plastic wrap.

STEP 13

Dye 30 ounces (850 g) of fondant black. Roll out to ¼ inch (6 mm) thick and cover the 6-inch (15 cm) tapered square tier. Smooth with the fondant smoother and trim off excess with the scissors and pizza cutter, saving the trimmings for making zebra stripes.

STEP 14

Dye 30 ounces (850 g) of fondant a light brown. Roll out to ¼ inch (6 mm) thick and cover the 8-inch (20 cm) tapered round tier. Smooth with the fondant smoother and trim off excess. Add the trimmings to the remaining fondant.

STEP 15

Dye the remaining fondant a dark brown. Roll out to ¼ inch (6 mm) thick and cover the 12-inch (30 cm) tapered square tier. Smooth with the fondant smoother and trim off excess. This tier should now be transfered to the 16-inch (40 cm) cake drum.

STEP 16

Cut 22 dowels to 3½ inches (9 cm) in length. Insert six dowels vertically through the cut-out hole into the 6-inch (15 cm) tier, eight through the hole into the 8-inch (20 cm) tier, and eight into the 12-inch (30 cm) tier. Stack the tiers. Sharpen two 12-inch (30 cm) long dowels. Drive them down vertically through the tiers, one on either side of the cake.

STEP 17

Using the veining tool, gently score the sides of the 12-inch (30 cm) square tier to give an alligator skin effect. Mix brown food coloring with vodka, and paint the entire tier. Using the same brown mixture, paint random spots of all shapes and sizes on the 8-inch (20 cm) round tier. Mix black coloring with vodka and add random black outlines to the brown spots to create the look of leopard spots. Paint the entire 6-inch (15 cm) tier with the black food coloring to make it shiny like leather.

STEP 18

Roll out the remaining black fondant to ⅛ inch (3 mm) thick. Use the pizza cutter to cut out tapered strips. Attach these strips to the 4-inch (10 cm) round tier to create zebra stripes. Using the leftover black fondant, roll out ¼-teaspoon (1 ml) balls. Arrange these balls along the base of the 4-inch (10 cm) round tier and the 8-inch (20 cm) round tier.

STEP 19

Fill the piping bag with black royal icing and, with the #12 tip, pipe dots on the base of the 6-inch (15 cm) square tier and the 12-inch (30 cm) square tier.

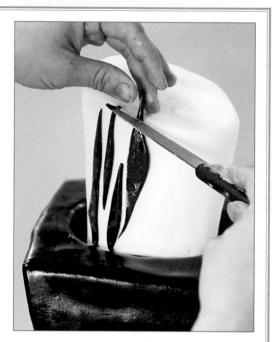

STREET SCENE

This miniature three-tiered cake will transport you to a tranquil street corner near a bakery. Let your imagination run wild when adding decorations. The details will amaze your guests. You will need to start one day early for all decorations to dry in time.

TOOLS

- serrated knife
- offset spatula
- 4-inch (10 cm) square cake board
- 5-inch (13 cm) square cake board
- 8-inch (20 cm) square cake board
- dough scraper
- pastry brush
- 12-inch (30 cm) square cake drum
- rolling pin
- pizza cutter
- plastic wrap
- fondant smoother
- cobblestone impression mat
- utility knife
- dowels and shears
- pencil sharpener
- ruler
- pencil
- parchment paper
- piping bag
- flower former
- wire
- small and large square cutters
- small and large round cutters
- small sharp knife
- small palette knife
- frill cutter
- small and large oval cutters
- toothpicks
- fine paintbrush
- scissors
- striped ribbon
- glue stick

MATERIALS

- 2 (4-inch/10 cm) square vanilla cakes (2 inches/ 5 cm high)
- 2 (5-inch/13 cm) square vanilla cakes (2 inches/ 5 cm high)
- 2 (8-inch/20 cm) square vanilla cakes (2 inches/ 5 cm high)
- 6½ cups (1.625 L) buttercream
- 80 oz. (2.3 kg) white fondant
- gel food coloring — black, blue, red, yellow, brown, pink, and ivory
- piping gel
- cornstarch
- royal icing
- black Candy Melts

OVERVIEW

This cake will require two days to complete.

DAY ONE
- Prepare the fondant and make the decorations for each tier (approx. 3 hrs.)

DAY TWO
- Make six cakes and set aside to cool (approx. 3 hrs.)
- Level, split, fill, and assemble the tiers (1½ hrs.)

- Cover each tier with buttercream (2½ hrs., including refrigeration)
- Cover the tiers with fondant (1½ hrs.)
- Cover tiers with cobblestone fondant (1½ hrs.)
- Decorate each tier (2½ hrs.)
- Assemble all the tiers (1 hr.)
- Final touches (½ hr.)

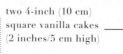

two 4-inch (10 cm) square vanilla cakes (2 inches/5 cm high)

two 5-inch (13 cm) square vanilla cakes (2 inches/5 cm high)

two 8-inch (20 cm) square vanilla cakes (2 inches/5 cm high)

STEP 1

Level the tops of all cakes, split them in half horizontally, and fill between the layers with buttercream, working with each tier on its corresponding cake board. Cover tiers with a thin layer of buttercream. Chill until firm. Cover with a second coat of buttercream and smooth with the dough scraper. Refrigerate for 1 hour.

STEP 2

Dye 10 ounces (280 g) of fondant black, 15 ounces (425 g) gray, 1 ounce (28 g) blue, 1 ounce (28 g) red, 1 ounce (28 g) yellow, 1 ounce (28 g) brown, 1 ounce (28 g) ivory, and 1 ounce (28 g) pink. Leave the remaining fondant white.

STEP 3

With the pastry brush, spread piping gel on the 12-inch (30 cm) cake drum. On a cornstarch-covered working surface, roll out the black fondant to ¼ inch (6 mm) thick. Cover the cake drum and trim the excess. Save the trimmings and cover them with plastic wrap.

STEP 4

Roll out the white fondant to ¼ inch (6 mm) thick and cover the 8-inch (20 cm) tier. Smooth with the fondant smoother. Trim off excess and save trimmings, covered with plastic wrap. Transfer the tier to the prepared cake drum.

STEP 5

Roll out the gray fondant to ¼ inch (6 mm) thick and cover the 5-inch (13 cm) tier. Smooth with the fondant smoother. Trim off excess and save trimmings, covered with plastic wrap. Repeat with the 4-inch (10 cm) tier.

STEP 6

Roll out the remaining gray fondant to ¼ inch (6 mm) thick. Place the impression mat on top and roll over the mat with the rolling pin. Lift off the mat, and you will see that the fondant now has the texture of cobblestones.

STEP 7

Cut out panels with the pizza cutter. Attach with a little water to one side of the 8-inch (20 cm) tier. Trim off excess with the utility knife. Do this until the four sides are covered. Repeat with the 4-inch (10 cm) and 5-inch (13 cm) tiers.

STEP 8

Cut ten 4-inch (10 cm) long dowels. Insert six vertically into the 8-inch (20 cm) tier and four into the 5-inch (13 cm) tier. Stack the 5-inch (13 cm) tier on top of the 8-inch (20 cm) tier and the 4-inch (10 cm) tier on top of the 5-inch (13 cm) tier. Sharpen one end of a 12-inch (30 cm) dowel and drive it vertically through the center of all three tiers.

STEP 9

With a ruler and pencil, draw four rectangles that are 1½ inches (4 cm) wide and 8 inches (20 cm) long on a piece of parchment paper. Also make four rectangles that are 1½ inches (4 cm) wide and 4 inches (10 cm) long. Dye royal icing black and fill the piping bag. Cut a small hole in a corner of the bag and pipe along the lines on the parchment paper. Pipe circles in the middle of each rectangle and a line through the middle horizontally. These will be the railings, which will go on top of the 4-inch (10 cm) tier and the 8-inch (20 cm) tier. Let dry.

STEP 10

To create two balconies, cover a flower former with plastic wrap. Pipe the same design on the flower former as you used to make the railings. Let dry.

STEP 11

To make lanterns, cut four pieces of wire 6 inches (15 cm) long. Using the shears, curl one end of the wire into a little hook. Measure out four ½-teaspoon (2 ml) balls of black fondant. Using your fingers, shape the balls into lanterns. Roll out the yellow fondant to 1/16 inch (2 mm) thick and cut out small squares. Attach to the sides of the lanterns and trim off the excess with the utility knife. Dip the hooked end of each wire into water, and insert into the tops of the lanterns. Set aside overnight to dry.

STEP 12

To make an awning, roll out the red fondant to ½ inch (1 cm) thick. Cut out a large circle with the round cutter. With a knife, cut off a third of the circle at the bottom. Use the palette knife to score lines into the remaining part of the circle (to give texture to the awning). Roll out the white fondant to ¹⁄₁₆ inch (2 mm) thick. Using the frill cutter, cut out a scalloped strip of white fondant. Attach it with a little water to the straight edge of the piece of red fondant.

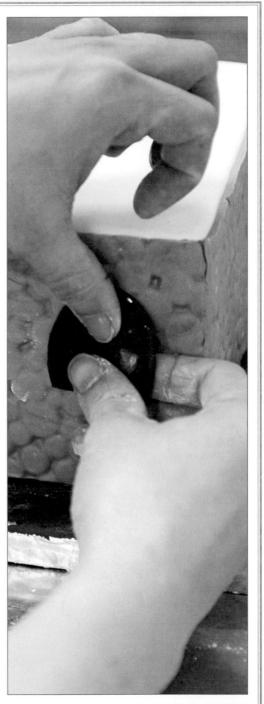

STEP 13

Roll out the remaining black fondant to $\frac{1}{16}$ inch (2 mm) thick. Using the appropriate cutters, cut out five large ovals and one large square. Also cut out two rectangles measuring 2 inches (5 cm) wide and 4 inches (10 cm) long.

With a little water, attach the square to one side of the 8-inch (20 cm) tier. This will be the front door. Cut a third off the bottom of each black oval, and attach one on either side of the door to simulate windows. Attach the remaining ovals to three sides of the second tier. Attach the two rectangles on opposite sides of the 8-inch (20 cm) tier.

STEP 14

Roll out the yellow fondant to ¹/₁₆ inch (2 mm) thick. Cut out four small ovals, and then cut off a third of the bottom of the ovals. Then cut the remaining pieces into four equal parts. Attach these pieces to the black windows to create the look of windowpanes.

STEP 16

Roll out the blue fondant and cut out a large oval. Cut it in half vertically. Use a small piece of plastic wrap to make the curtain look like it is billowing. Allow to dry overnight. Attach it to the black oval of the front window on the second tier.

STEP 15

With toothpicks, attach the red awning to the top of the front door.

STEP 17

Roll out the remaining white fondant to
$^1/_{16}$ inch (2 mm) thick. Cut out two rectangles,
each 1½ inches (4 cm) wide by 3 inches (8 cm)
long. Attach these with a little water to the black
rectangles. These will be the display windows of
your bakery. Cut out cake shapes from the pink
and ivory fondant. Attach to the window with a
little water.

STEP 18

Measure out ¼ teaspoon (1 ml) of black
fondant. Shape with your fingers into a
weathervane. Attach to a toothpick and insert
it vertically into the center of the top tier.

STEP 19

Melt a little bit of black Candy Melts in a cone
made of parchment paper. Carefully remove the
railings from the parchment paper. Attach them
to the top of the 8-inch (20 cm) tier with the
melted candy. Carefully remove the balconies
from the flower former and attach them to the
windows without curtains on the second tier.

STEP 20

Roll out the white fondant to ¼ inch (6 mm) thickness. Cut out four small circles. With a fine paintbrush and black food coloring, paint the numbers and hands on the clocks. Roll out brown fondant to ⅛ inch (3 mm) thick. Cut out four rectangles measuring 1½ inches (4 cm) wide and 3 inches (8 cm) long. Cut out a circle from each rectangle with the circle cutter used for the clocks. Score each brown piece with a small palette knife for texture. These are your shutters. Attach the clocks to the building. Attach the shutters to the sides of each clock.

STEP 21

Attach the railings to the top of the 4-inch (10 cm) tier with some Candy Melts. Insert the wires of the lanterns into each corner of the cake drum. Cut the striped ribbon to your desired size and attach it to the cake drum with the glue stick.

WEDDING GOWN

At every wedding, the focus is on the bride's gown and the wedding cake.
What happens when the cake mimics the gown?

TOOLS

- large pastry brush
- 14-inch (35 cm)
  round cake drum
- rolling pin
- sharp knife
- serrated knife
- offset spatula
- 6-inch (15 cm)
  round cake board
- 2 (8-inch/20 cm)
  round cake boards
- 10-inch (25 cm)
  round cake board
- dowels and shears
- dough scraper
- fondant smoother
- pizza cutter
- plastic wrap
- medium leaf cutter
- piece of thin foam
- round stick
- paintbrush
- fondant ribbon cutter
- pencil sharpener
- ivory satin ribbon
- glue stick

MATERIALS

- piping gel
- 100 oz. (2.8 kg) white fondant
- cornstarch
- 2 (6-inch/15 cm) round
  vanilla cakes (2 inches/
  5 cm high)
- 1 (8-inch/20 cm) round
  vanilla cake (2 inches/
  5 cm high)
- 3 (10-inch/25 cm) round
  vanilla cakes (2 inches/
  5 cm high)
- 12 cups (3 L) buttercream
- fine and medium silver
  dragées or fondant beads
- medium pearl dragées or
  fondant beads
- gum paste

OVERVIEW

This cake will require two days to complete.

DAY ONE
- Prepare the cake drum
  and cover with fondant
  (15 mins.)

- Make the six cakes and set
  aside to cool (approx.
  3 hrs.)

- Level, split, fill, and
  assemble each tier (1 hr.)

- Cover tiers with
  buttercream (1½ hrs.,
  including refrigeration)

- Cover all tiers with
  fondant (½ hr.)

- Cover the 8-inch (20 cm)
  tier with silver dragées
  (10 mins.)

DAY TWO
- Prepare the fondant leaves
  and attach to the 10-inch
  (25 cm) tier (approx. 3 hrs.)

- Prepare, make, and
  attach the fondant strips
  and buttons to the 6-inch
  (15 cm) tier (2 hrs.)

- Insert dowels and
  assemble the tiers (½ hr.)

- Final touches (10 mins.)

two 6-inch (15 cm)
round vanilla cakes
(2 inches/5 cm high)

one 8-inch (20 cm)
round vanilla cake
(2 inches/5 cm high)

three 10-inch (25 cm)
round vanilla cakes
(2 inches/5 cm high)

STEP 1

With the pastry brush, spread piping gel evenly over the cake drum. On a cornstarch-covered surface, roll out 10 ounces (280 g) of the white fondant to ¼ inch (6 mm) thick and cover the cake drum. Trim the excess with the sharp knife.

STEP 2

Prepare the 6-inch (15 cm) and 8-inch (20 cm) tiers by leveling their tops with the serrated knife, splitting them in half horizontally, and filling between the layers with buttercream. Place each tier on its corresponding cake board. Cover both tiers with a thin layer of buttercream. You will have one 4-inch (10 cm) high tier and one 2-inch (5 cm) high tier.

STEP 3

For the 10-inch (25 cm) tier, level all three cake rounds and split them in half horizontally. Fill between the layers with buttercream. Stack just two of the cake rounds (four layers of cake in total) on the 10-inch (25 cm) board. Cut six pieces of dowel to 3 inches (8 cm) long, and insert them vertically into the filled 10-inch (25 cm) cake. Spread a layer of buttercream on top. Place the remaining 8-inch (20 cm) round cake board in the center. Fill between the layers of the remaining 10-inch (25 cm) cake round with buttercream and stack it on top. The result will be a 10-inch (25 cm) tier measuring 6 inches (15 cm).

STEP 4

Cut another six pieces of dowel to 3 inches (8 cm) in length. Insert the dowels vertically into the top half of the stacked 10-inch (25 cm) tier.

STEP 5

Spread a thin layer of buttercream on all three tiers. Refrigerate for 20 minutes. Cover the top and sides with a second, thicker coat of buttercream. Smooth with the dough scraper and refrigerate for 1 hour.

STEP 6

Roll out all the remaining white fondant to ¼ inch (6 mm) thick. Cover all three tiers. Smooth with the fondant smoother and trim the excess with the pizza cutter. Save the trimmings, wrapped in plastic wrap. Transfer the 10-inch (25 cm) tier to the cake drum, securing in place with a dab of royal icing.

STEP 7

Roll out the leftover fondant to ⅛ inch (3 mm) thick. Using the medium leaf cutter, cut out medium-sized leaves.

STEP 8

Working on one leaf at a time, place the leaves on the thin piece of foam and thin the edges with the round stick.

STEP 9

Starting from the base and working your way up, attach the leaves to the side of the 10-inch (25 cm) tier with water. Cover the entire tier, leaving an 8-inch (20 cm) diameter on the top, where the second tier will sit.

STEP 10

Mix 1 teaspoon (1 ml) of gum paste with ¼ cup (60 ml) of water to make an edible "glue." Brush the side of the 8-inch (20 cm) tier with this glue. Holding the tier at an angle, sprinkle the side with the fine silver dragées or fondant beads. Try to coat the sides as thoroughly as you can. Fill in the gaps without silver dragées with the pearl dragées or fondant beads.

STEP 11

Roll out the remaining white fondant to $1/8$-inch (3-mm) thickness. With the fondant ribbon cutter, cut 1-inch- (2.5 cm) wide strips that are long enough to wrap around the 6-inch (15 cm) tier. Moisten half of the strip lengthwise with water. Fold it over so that the strip is ½ inch (1 cm) wide.

STEP 12

With the seam facing out, attach the strip to the top of the 6-inch (15 cm) tier with a little water. Allow the ends to overlap and trim the excess with a knife.

STEP 13

Roll ½ teaspoon (2 ml) of fondant into a ball to form a button. Attach with a little water where the ends of the strip overlap.

STEP 14

Repeat until the entire tier is encircled with strips of fondant and you have a row of buttons down the front side.

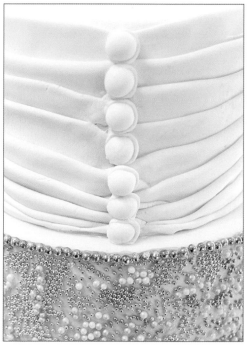

STEP 15

Cut six pieces of dowel to a length of 2 inches (5 cm), insert them vertically into the 8-inch (20 cm) tier. Leave a small space of 2 inches (5 cm) from the edge. Place a dab of royal icing on top of the dowels. Set the 8-inch (20 cm) tier on top of the 10-inch (25 cm) tier. Then, set the 6-inch (15 cm) tier on top of the 8-inch (20 cm) tier. Sharpen one end of a 12-inch (30 cm) long dowel. Drive it vertically into the center of all three tiers. Cover the hole on top with some royal icing.

STEP 16

Using royal icing, attach medium silver dragées or fondant beads to the top edge and base of the second tier. Attach the ivory ribbon to the cake drum with the glue stick.

INDEX

CREDITS

Unless specified, all images are the copyright of
Quintet Publishing Ltd, and may not be reproduced
without prior written permission. While every
effort has been made to credit contributors, Quintet
Publishing would like to apologize should there have
been any omissions or errors—and would be pleased
to make the appropriate correction for future editions
of the book.